BestMasters

Springer awards „BestMasters" to the best master's theses which have been completed at renowned Universities in Germany, Austria, and Switzerland.
The studies received highest marks and were recommended for publication by supervisors. They address current issues from various fields of research in natural sciences, psychology, technology, and economics.
The series addresses practitioners as well as scientists and, in particular, offers guidance for early stage researchers.

Tobias Kranz

Persistent Stochastic Shocks in a New Keynesian Model with Uncertainty

Springer Gabler

Tobias Kranz
Trier, Germany

Master Thesis, University of Trier 2015

BestMasters
ISBN 978-3-658-15638-1 ISBN 978-3-658-15639-8 (eBook)
DOI 10.1007/978-3-658-15639-8

Library of Congress Control Number: 2016954031

Springer Gabler

Printed on acid-free paper

This Springer Gabler imprint is published by Springer Nature
The registered company is Springer Fachmedien Wiesbaden GmbH
The registered company address is: Abraham-Lincoln-Str. 46, 65189 Wiesbaden, Germany

Acknowledgements

I would like to take this opportunity to thank several people who have supported me during the two years of my master studies and been of great help in the work on this thesis.

I highly value all the input Jun. Prof. Dr. Matthias Neuenkirch has given me. He answered every one of my questions swiftly and thoughtfully. I admire his work ethics and thank him for guiding me through this process in such a supportive manner. Furthermore, I would like to thank Stefan Geisen for his great mathematical help in past projects and for the many fruitful conversations we had on the topics of economics and mathematics. I would also like to express my gratitude to Sarah Cames for developing and improving my English skills and for being so diligent in correcting my mistakes.

Finally, I wish to thank my family for their endless support and encouragement, not only throughout my studies, but throughout my whole life.

Tobias Kranz

Trier, November 2015

Contents

List of Figures

List of Tables

Lists of Symbols and Acronyms

Table 1: Greek Alphabet

Letter	Description
α	Summarizing parameters ($\alpha_\gamma, \alpha_y, \alpha_\pi, \alpha_\mu, \alpha_e, \alpha_\sigma$)
β	Discount factor (time preference)
γ	Parameter in cost function
δ	Weighting on output gap in loss function
ε	Elasticity of substitution
ζ	Error term of cost shock
η	Error term of demand shock
θ	Auxiliary parameter
κ	Slope of NKPC
λ	Lagrange variable (multiplier); Eigenvalue
μ	Cost shock persistence
ν	Demand shock persistence
ξ	Integration variable
π	Inflation
σ	Reciprocal value of the IES
σ_e^2	Cost shock variance
σ_u^2	Demand shock variance
τ	Firm index
ϕ	Price stickiness
χ	Lagrange variable (multiplier)
ψ	Lagrange variable (multiplier)

Table 2: Latin Alphabet

Letter	Description
c	Constants in cost function (c_{fix}, c_{var})
e	Cost shock
i	Nominal interest rate; Imaginary number
j	Control variable
k	Cost parameter in Calvo pricing
n	Natural number
p	Log-linearized price around the steady state
q	Parameter in the generalized mean formula
r	Long-run real interest rate
s	Control variable in intertemporal optimizations
ss	Notation for *steady state* (long-term value)
t	Time variable
u	Demand shock
x	Calvo price
y	Log-linearized output growth rate around the steady state
$\widehat{y}$	Growth rate of output gap around the steady state
$\widetilde{y}$	Output growth rate
z	Example for a log-linearized variable
A	Vectors in a system of difference equations (A_0, A_t, A_{t+1})
B	Bonds
C	Consumption
$K(.)$	Cost function
$\mathscr{L}(.)$	Lagrange function
M	Coefficient matrix
P	Price; Price level
$U(.)$	Utility function
$V(.)$	Value function in Bellman equation
W	Wage
Y	Output
Z	Example variable

Table 3: Abbreviations

Abbr.	Term
AD	Aggregated Demand
AR	Autoregressive
AS	Aggregated Supply
BL	Baseline
CES	Constant Elasticity of Substitution
DSGE	Dynamic Stochastic General Equilibrium
ECB	European Central Bank
GDP	Gross Domestic Product
IES	Intertemporal Elasticity of Substitution
IS	Investment/Saving
MATLAB	Matrix Laboratory
NKM	New Keynesian Model
NKPC	New Keynesian Phillips Curve
RBC	Real Business Cycle

1 Introduction

The main objective of this paper is to examine a dynamic general equilibrium condition out of a basic three-equation New Keynesian model (NKM), augmented with stochastic terms and non-linearity. More precisely, the additive terms behave like persistent stochastic shocks and are modeled as an exogenous first-order autoregressive process. In line with the literature (see, among others, the textbooks by Galí 2015 and Walsh 2010) cost shock and demand shock are utilized for the New Keynesian Phillips curve (NKPC) and the forward-looking IS curve respectively. Non-linearity enters the model through a second-order Taylor approximation regarding the IS curve. Bauer and Neuenkirch (2015) were the first to derive such a framework and found empirical evidence that central banks indeed take the resulting uncertainty into account. Moreover, their paper provides strong arguments that linear macroeconomic models are a shortcoming in the scientific literature.

The analysis is preceded by an overview of dynamic stochastic general equilibrium (DSGE) models with the evolution of the Real business cycle (RBC) theory and the New Keynesian framework resulting in the New neoclassical synthesis. First, in the analytical part, demand and supply side (including monopolistic competition and price rigidity) will yield the NKPC, the New Keynesian contribution to the framework. Second, from the household's Euler equation follows the forward-looking IS curve, originating in the RBC theory. Third, the central bank's optimization under discretion ends in a (standard) targeting rule.

The rest of the thesis consists of the augmentation with shocks and uncertainty. After checking the uniqueness of the equilibrium and the derivation of the equilibrium condition, initially without uncertainty, the examination is going to be conducted both analytically via differentials and as numerical simulation in MATLAB. A thorough literature research discusses possible parameter ranges, with a focus on the persistence parameter. Furthermore, strict inflation targeting is considered. In a very similar way, the quadratic approximation of the IS curve is dealt with. In addition, the case without certainty-equivalence and persistence is going to be taken into consideration. In a last step, all results will be compared and interpreted in the context of crisis scenarios, booms or relatively tranquil times. The comparison of models and settings is of great importance, rather than noting absolute values.

To keep the framework easily understandable, government, investments, money supply, and labor markets are omitted. Consequently, neither money holdings nor working hours (or leisure time) will enter the household's utility function. I also attach a great deal of importance to the compelling nature and a clear step-by-step derivation of the NKM.

That is why, to the best of my knowledge, graduate readers will receive a comprehensive and comprehensible introduction to this state-of-the-art framework.

The remainder of this thesis is organized as follows: Section 2 reviews the NKM evolution and derives a basic version. Section 3 expands this with shocks, discusses the equilibrium condition, and simulates the results. Section 4 adds uncertainty to the model, simulates, and compares the findings with those in Section 3. Section 5 concludes.

2 New Keynesian Model

Years before the components of the New Keynesian framework were developed or used, there was already a major turning point in macroeconomic modelling, initiated by the prominent Lucas critique. Lucas (1976) denounced the shortcomings of economic policies that try to exploit relationships on the basis of (highly aggregated) historical data, such as the Phillips curve. As a reaction, households and firms would adapt (or even become forward-looking) and relationships could change or, in the case of the Phillips curve, break down.

The following historical recapitulation starts in the early 1980's and describes how the different NKM's origins have developed and coalesced since. Subsequently, the theoretical part will be introduced including the NKPC (i.e., demand side, supply side, and Calvo pricing), the forward-looking IS curve, and a monetary policy rule under discretion.

2.1 The New Neoclassical Synthesis

The paper by Kydland and Prescott (1982) is considered to be the starting point in RBC theory. They explained fluctuations in business cycles with a non-time-separable utility function and focussed on intertemporal substitution. Prescott (1986) added shocks to technology and examined people's willingness and ability to intertemporally and intratemporally substitute in detail. Generally, the RBC theory established the use of fully specified DSGE models with characteristic features as the efficiency of business cycles, the importance of technology shocks (as a source of fluctuations in economic output), and the limited role of monetary factors (see Galí 2015, 2–3).

During the same time, in the 1980's, models with market imperfections were developed. Akerlof and Yellen (1985) gave an explanation of why variations in the nominal supply of money are not neutral in the short run. They emphasized the suboptimal reactions to demand shocks through price (and wage) inertia and that it is important to implement this property in RBC models. Mankiw (1985) discussed the conflict between modern neoclassical and traditional Keynesian theories. He modeled price inertia with fix costs (menu costs) and also assumed a monopoly, another market friction the RBC theory neglected. Blanchard and Kiyotaki (1987) came to the result that monopolistic competition, together with other imperfections, can explain why aggregated demand affects output.

The first derivation of a NKPC can be found in the paper by Roberts (1995, 979). Neither the name nor the mathematical methods (i.a. Calvo pricing) have fundamentally changed since. Early (complete) New Keynesian frameworks were modeled by Yun (1996) and Rotemberg and Woodford (1997). The latter explicitly referenced the Lucas critique and discussed the new era of macroeconomic models. In the same year, Goodfried and King (1997) proposed four elements typical for the combination of NKMs and RBC theory: Intertemporal optimization, rational expectations, imperfect competition, and costly price adjustment. They labeled it New neoclassical synthesis, in reference to the Neoclassical synthesis, which was developed and popularized in the decades after Keynes' main work and combined Keynesian macroeconomics with neoclassical thoughts.

In a next step, Clarida et al (2000) combined these thoughts and made big strides in the field of monetary policy. They surveyed the post-war United States economy in terms of forward-looking monetary policy implications. For their baseline model, they referenced i.a. Yun's paper and work by Woodford. As soon as DSGE models proved themselves to be capable of describing and explaining short-run fluctuations, price stickiness, and evaluating monetary policy; central banks adopted this and developed large-scale models. The most notable representative is the DSGE model by Smets and Wouters (2002), providing a theoretical foundation for the work done by the ECB.

The widely respected paper by Christiano et al (2005) showed that stickiness in nominal wages is more important than price sluggishness. By that time, these models included common features like households' habit persistence, that describes how past consumption influences the marginal utility of present consumption. Furthermore, they included Calvo pricing in both wages and prices, variable capital utilization, costs for capital adjustment, and a variety of shocks. These models implicate a monetary policy that is aimed to stabilize the economy. Generally, stabilizing inflation is sufficient, since a stabilized output goes hand in hand with maintaining perfectly stable inflation rates. In the article by Blanchard and Galí (2007), this property was named the "divine coincidence".

In the process evolving over the past decades, the main purpose was to understand (i) fluctuations, (ii) rigidities, and (iii) monetary policy, which can affect real output in the short run. Therefore, the New Keynesian framework provides the theoretical basis for much of the contemporary macroeconomic modeling.

2.2 New Keynesian Phillips Curve

For deriving the NKPC, two optimization problems concerning private households and firms are employed, leading to aggregated demand and supply. Furthermore, price rigidity is modeled through the method introduced by Calvo (1983). The time index t is only used from the Calvo Pricing section onwards, where it is needed to make a distinction between the different periods.

Demand Side

On the demand side, the representative consumer can choose from a variety of goods C_ξ which results in an average consumption of C. Usually, the CES function is used to model monopolistic competition[1], one of the two market frictions incorporated into the NKPC:

$$C = \left(\int_0^1 C_\xi^{\frac{\varepsilon-1}{\varepsilon}} \, d\xi \right)^{\frac{\varepsilon}{\varepsilon-1}}. \tag{1}$$

Here, $\xi \in [0,1]$ can be viewed as a continuum of firms from 0 to 100%. The exponent is a measure for the substitutability between the goods C_ξ, where ε represents the elasticity of substitution. A change in ε would result in a different mean for C.[2] Bauer and Neuenkirch (2015, 5) assume $\varepsilon > 1$, constant over time and common amongst all economic subjects.

A Hicksian-like[3] optimization by means of the Lagrangian function helps to solve for the demand curve:

$$\mathscr{L}(C_\xi, \lambda) = \int_0^1 P_\xi \cdot C_\xi \, d\xi - \lambda \left(\left(\int_0^1 C_\xi^{\frac{\varepsilon-1}{\varepsilon}} \, d\xi \right)^{\frac{\varepsilon}{\varepsilon-1}} - C \right). \tag{2}$$

Since firms have pricing power, the representative consumer takes prices P_ξ as given. Minimizing expenditures $\int P_\xi C_\xi$ with the constraint of a certain consumption level C requires the following first-order conditions[4] :

$$\frac{\partial \mathscr{L}}{\partial C_\tau} = P_\tau - \lambda C_\tau^{-\frac{1}{\varepsilon}} \left(\int_0^1 C_\xi^{\frac{\varepsilon-1}{\varepsilon}} \, d\xi \right)^{\frac{1}{\varepsilon-1}} = 0 \tag{3.1}$$

$$\frac{\partial \mathscr{L}}{\partial \lambda} = \left(\int_0^1 C_\xi^{\frac{\varepsilon-1}{\varepsilon}} \, d\xi \right)^{\frac{\varepsilon}{\varepsilon-1}} - C = 0. \tag{3.2}$$

[1] Dixit and Stiglitz (1977) developed this approach. However, they used a discrete sum and no integral but received the same results.

[2] Eq.(1) is an integral notation for the generalized mean $\bar{x} = \left(\frac{1}{n} \sum_{j=1}^{n} x_j^q \right)^{1/q}$ with $q = \frac{\varepsilon-1}{\varepsilon}$. See Appendix A.1 for a more detailed comparison.

[3] Since Hicksian demand will be determined by minimizing expenditures with a utility constraint, the present optimization problem will transfer to this type using the simple utility function $U(C) = C$.

[4] Note that τ denotes a continuum of derivatives.

Differentiating with respect to λ provides the constraint, Eq.(1). Rearranging[5] (3.1) and defining $\lambda \equiv P$[6] as the aggregated price level yields

$$C_\tau = \left(\frac{P}{P_\tau}\right)^\varepsilon C, \tag{4}$$

the demand[7] for good i. Substituting this in Eq.(1) and rearranging[8] gives the formula

$$P = \left(\int_0^1 P_\xi^{1-\varepsilon}\, d\xi\right)^{\frac{1}{1-\varepsilon}}, \tag{5}$$

which describes the aggregated price level[9]. The lack of investment and governmental spendings in this model leads to $Y_\tau = C_\tau$. Each firms' production Y_τ will be consumed completely by private households and hence $Y = C$. Eq.(4) can now be written in the aggregated demand form

$$Y_\tau = \frac{1}{P_\tau^\varepsilon} \cdot Y P^\varepsilon, \tag{6}$$

that takes the shape of a hyperbola and is, in consequence, very similar to the traditional downward sloping AD curve.[10]

Supply Side

Each firm takes the aggregated demand function and the aggregated price level P as given since any single firm is too small to directly influence other prices or productions. It chooses its own price P_τ and faces the typical (real) profit maximization problem

$$\max_{P_\tau, Y_\tau} \left\{ \frac{P_\tau Y_\tau}{P} - K(Y_\tau) \right\}, \tag{7}$$

[5]See Appendix A.3 for more details.

[6]There are good reasons for this step. When the consumption constraint is relaxed by one unit, total consumption expenditures (see Galí (2015, 53)) will increase to $(C+1)P = CP + P$, where P is the amount by which the optimum will change. This is exactly the information the Lagrange multiplier λ contains. See Chiang and Wainwright (2005, 353–354) for a detailed proof with λ expressed as a derivative.

[7]It is straightforward to show that ε is in fact the elasticity of substitution. Dividing two demand functions (for goods a and b) by each other results in $(C_b/C_a) = (P_a/P_b)^\varepsilon$. Since ε is defined as the percentage change in relative goods by a percentage change in relative prices, this is exactly what the equation shows. See Chiang and Wainwright (2005, 396–399) for the definition and the case of the CES production function.

[8]See Appendix A.4 for more details.

[9]Again, like Eq.(1), this can be examined through the generalized mean, see Appendix A.5.

[10]The concise paper of Kyer and Maggs (1992) recapitulates the topic and analytically derives an AD curve consisting of both the Keynes and the Pigou effect.

where it substracts the real costs K from the real revenue. Using (6) and rearranging leads to

$$\max_{P_\tau} \left\{ \left(\frac{P_\tau}{P}\right)^{1-\varepsilon} Y - K\left(\left(\frac{P_\tau}{P}\right)^{-\varepsilon} Y\right) \right\}. \tag{8}$$

The first-order condition is now straightforward, using the chain rule:

$$\frac{\partial}{\partial P_\tau} = (1-\varepsilon)\left(\frac{P_\tau}{P}\right)^{-\varepsilon} \cdot \frac{Y}{P} - K'(Y_\tau)\cdot(-\varepsilon)\left(\frac{P_\tau}{P}\right)^{-\varepsilon-1} \cdot \frac{Y}{P} = 0. \tag{9}$$

Simplifying and denoting the optimal price with P_τ^* yields

$$(\varepsilon - 1)\left(\frac{P_\tau^*}{P}\right)^{-\varepsilon} = K'(Y_\tau)\cdot\varepsilon\left(\frac{P_\tau^*}{P}\right)^{-\varepsilon-1} \tag{10.1}$$

$$\Leftrightarrow \qquad 1 = \left(\frac{\varepsilon}{\varepsilon-1}\right) K'(Y_\tau)\left(\frac{P_\tau^*}{P}\right)^{-1} \tag{10.2}$$

$$\Leftrightarrow \qquad P_\tau^* = \left(\frac{\varepsilon}{\varepsilon-1}\right) K'(Y_\tau)\cdot P, \tag{10.3}$$

an important result that states that the optimal price P_τ^* equals the nominal marginal costs and a mark-up $(\varepsilon/(\varepsilon-1)) > 1$ for all $\varepsilon > 1$. However, perfect substitutes let the monopolistic structure vanish and show the typical polypolistic result:

$$\lim_{\varepsilon\to\infty}\left(\frac{\varepsilon}{\varepsilon-1}\right) K'(Y_\tau)\cdot P = K'(Y_\tau)\cdot P = P_\tau^*. \tag{11}$$

Now, with a cost function in real terms of quantities Y_τ defined[11] as

$$K(Y_\tau) = \frac{c_{var}}{\gamma+1} Y_\tau^{\gamma+1} + c_{fix}, \tag{12}$$

where c_{fix} are the fix costs, c_{var} is a measure for the variable costs and γ represents the elasticity of marginal costs, (10.3) becomes a micro-funded AS curve that takes the form of a power function:

$$P_\tau^* = \left(\frac{\varepsilon}{\varepsilon-1}\right) c_{var} Y_\tau^{\gamma}\cdot P. \tag{13}$$

Log-linearization. It is convenient to use log-linearized variables instead of level variables to be able to solve the model analytically. Also, some interpretations of the

[11] Bauer and Neuenkirch (2015, 6) showed that an explicit formulation of the cost function is not necessary. However, to give a better understanding of the mechanics behind the NKPC, an actual function is used.

results, in terms of elasticity and growth rates, become quite useful.[12] So both (6) and (13) will now be approximated through log-linearization around the steady state.[13] But first some preparation is necessary.

Let Z be a state variable that can change over time and Z_{ss} its long-term value. When defining

$$z \equiv \ln Z - \ln Z_{ss}, \tag{14}$$

z becomes a good approximation of $\widehat{z}$, the growth rate around the steady state.[14] Furthermore, in the steady state, long-term values for individual variables are by definition the same as for those on aggregated level, thus $Z_{\tau ss} = Z_{ss}$. The state would otherwise include endogenous forces. And finally, the long-run marginal costs equal the multiplicative inverse of the firms' mark-up:[15]

$$c_{var} Y_{ss}^{\gamma} = \frac{\varepsilon - 1}{\varepsilon}. \tag{15}$$

An explanation for that would be the long-run version of Eq.(13) and hence $P_{\tau ss} = P_{ss}$. Now this can be applied to the previous results. First, Eq.(6), the AD curve will be log-linearized. Taking logs, expanding with the log long-term values, and using (14) gives

$$\ln Y_\tau = \ln Y + \varepsilon(\ln P - \ln P_\tau) \tag{16.1}$$
$$\Leftrightarrow \quad \ln Y_\tau - \ln Y = -\varepsilon(\ln P_\tau - \ln P) \tag{16.2}$$
$$\Leftrightarrow \quad \ln Y_\tau - \ln Y_{ss} - (\ln Y - \ln Y_{ss}) = -\varepsilon(\ln P_\tau - \ln P_{ss} - (\ln P - \ln P_{ss})) \tag{16.3}$$
$$\Leftrightarrow \quad y_\tau - y = -\varepsilon(p_\tau - p) \tag{16.4}$$
$$\Leftrightarrow \quad y_\tau = -\varepsilon p_\tau + \varepsilon p + y, \tag{16.5}$$

a linearized AD curve in terms of growth rates with the slope of $-1/\varepsilon$. A higher elasticity of substitution would result in a flatter curve, so a change in the firm's price growth p_τ would have a stronger effect on production growth y_τ.

[12] See Romer (2012, 207), Judd (1998, 200–202), the paper by Uhlig (1999), and the guide by Zietz (2008).

[13] The approximation becomes more precise with smaller growth rates, that is exactly what the steady state can offer. Judd (1998, 196–198) provides a goodness of fit comparison.

[14] See Appendix A.6 for a detailed calculation regarding $\widehat{z}$ and the actual growth rates $\widetilde{z}$ from one period to the next. Incidentally, there is no need to use $\widetilde{z}$ in the basic model. Furthermore, a first-order Taylor approximation "in reverse" shows the relationship between z and $\widehat{z}$:
$\widehat{z} \approx \ln(1+\widehat{z}) = \ln\left(1 + \frac{Z - Z_{ss}}{Z_{ss}}\right) = \ln\left(1 + \frac{Z}{Z_{ss}} - 1\right) = \ln\left(\frac{Z}{Z_{ss}}\right) = \ln Z - \ln Z_{ss} \equiv z.$

[15] Other authors simply define this property, see e.g. Galí (2015, 57).

Next, with the use of (15), the AS curve type Eq.(13), can be rewritten in a similar way:

$$\ln P^*_\tau = \ln\left(\frac{\varepsilon}{\varepsilon-1}\right) + \ln c_{var} + \gamma \ln Y_\tau + \ln P \tag{17.1}$$

$$\Leftrightarrow \quad \ln P^*_\tau - \ln P = \ln\left(\frac{\varepsilon}{\varepsilon-1}\right) + \ln c_{var} + \gamma\left(\ln Y_\tau - \ln Y_{ss} + \ln Y_{ss}\right) \tag{17.2}$$

$$\Leftrightarrow \quad p^*_\tau - p = \gamma y_\tau + \ln\left(\frac{\varepsilon}{\varepsilon-1}\right) + \ln c_{var} + \gamma \ln Y_{ss} \tag{17.3}$$

$$\Leftrightarrow \quad p^*_\tau - p = \gamma y_\tau + \ln\left(c_{var} Y^\gamma_{ss}\right) - \ln\left(\frac{\varepsilon-1}{\varepsilon}\right) \tag{17.4}$$

$$\Leftrightarrow \quad p^*_\tau - p = \gamma y_\tau + \underbrace{\ln\left(\frac{c_{var} Y^\gamma_{ss}}{(\varepsilon-1)/\varepsilon}\right)}_{=0}. \tag{17.5}$$

The latter expression shows the assumption that the log deviations of marginal costs from their long-run trend values are linear in the amount of γ. When the firm's optimized price growth p^*_τ is equal to the aggregated price growth p, then there is no growth in the firm's production. Having log-linearized both demand and supply side, Figure 1 sums up.

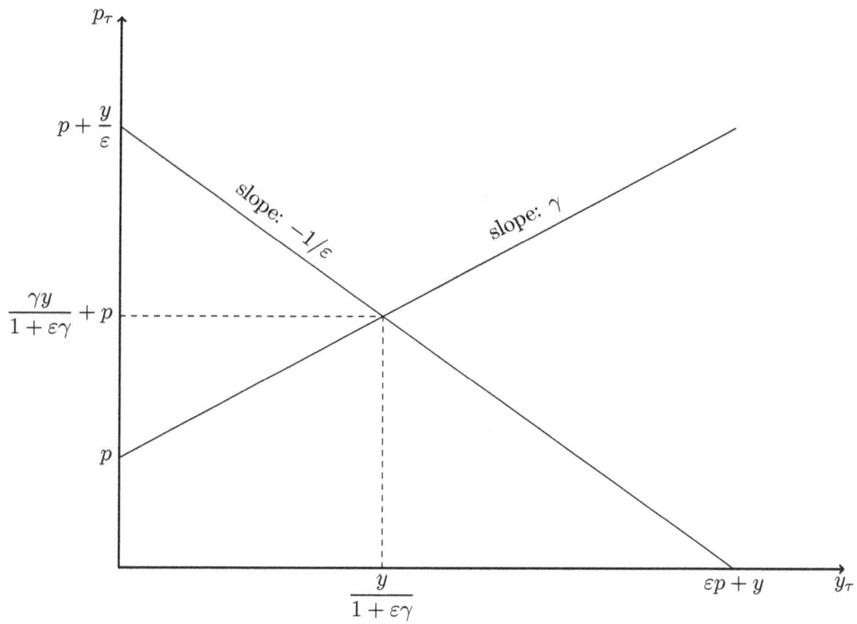

Figure 1: Graphical results of households' and firms' static optimization.

Finally, inserting (16.5) in (17.5) combines all the results and gives

$$
\begin{aligned}
& & p_\tau^* - p &= \gamma(-\varepsilon p_\tau^* + \varepsilon p + y) && (18.1)\\
&\Leftrightarrow & p_\tau^* - p &= -\gamma\varepsilon(p_\tau^* - p) + \gamma y && (18.2)\\
&\Leftrightarrow & (1+\gamma\varepsilon)(p_\tau^* - p) &= \gamma y && (18.3)\\
&\Leftrightarrow & p_\tau^* - p &= \left(\frac{\gamma}{1+\gamma\varepsilon}\right) y. && (18.4)
\end{aligned}
$$

Recalling that y can be approximated with $\widehat{y}$, the GDP growth rate around the steady state, and using $\alpha_\gamma \in [0, 1[$ as a summarizing parameter, Eq.(18.4) yields

$$p_\tau^* - p = \alpha_\gamma \widehat{y}, \qquad (19)$$

a description of the steady state output growth rate, depending on price growth and microeconomic behavior. The next section introduces a non-optimal price setting scheme which replicates the actual observed economic patterns.[16]

Calvo Pricing

Nominal rigidities as the second market friction in the basic NKM are implemented through the assumption that the firms' infrequent price adjustment follows an exogenous Poisson process[17], where all firms have a constant probability (ϕ) to be unable to update their price in each period with $\phi \in [0, 1[$ (i.e., $\phi = 0$ in the absence of price rigidity). It is crucial that price-setters do not know how long the nominal price will remain in place. Only the expected value is known due to probabilities that are all equal and constant for all firms and periods. This implies a probability of ϕ^j for having the same price in j periods as today and so the average expected duration between price changes will be $1/(1-\phi)$.[18]

From now on, the time index t will be used, as more than one period is being considered. Simultaniously, the firm index τ is no longer important since it is sufficient to calculate with a share of firms ϕ (or $1-\phi$). Hence, $p_\tau^* \equiv p_t^*$ and $p \equiv p_t$. When x_t is the

---

[16]See the survey by Taylor (1999), that came to abundant evidence. See also Galí (2015, 7–8) for a literature overview.

[17]Calvo (1983) originally wrote his article in continuous time. However, using discrete periods immensely helps the clearness and is more realistic with regard to how the central bank actually operates. Moreover, Calvo (1983, 396–397) shows the equivalence of both approaches. An alternative model of sticky prices was provided by Rotemberg (1982). See also Ascari and Rossi (2008) for a comparison of both approaches in the context of the NKPC.

[18]See Appendix A.7 for proof.

price that firms will set in period t (provided they are able to do so), the following will apply:

$$p_t = \underbrace{\phi p_{t-1}}_{\text{share of } \textit{sticky prices}} + \underbrace{(1-\phi)x_t}_{\text{share of price adjuster}} \tag{20.1}$$

$$\Leftrightarrow \quad x_t = \frac{p_t - \phi p_{t-1}}{1-\phi} \tag{20.2}$$

$$\Rightarrow \quad E_t x_{t+1} = \frac{E_t p_{t+1} - \phi p_t}{1-\phi}. \tag{20.3}$$

Firms will act on the probability of not being able to adjust prices in future periods. In consequence, they try to set a price x_t that is not necessarily the optimal price p_t^*, derived in the previous section. Also, in the presence of price rigidities, $x_t \neq p_t^*$ generally holds.

To reveal the mechanics behind the staggered price setting, it is convenient to verbally treat p_t and x_t as level variables. Strictly speaking, the firms set price growth paths in the following optimization problem rather than maximizing a discounted profit as the difference between revenue and costs[19]. This is due to the fact that it is more in line with the other microfoundations in the model. In the present way, the optimal reset price, determined by the discounted sum of future profits, is derived through a quadratic approximation of the per-period deviation from maximum-possible profit with $\beta \in [0, 1[$, the discount factor over an infinite planning horizon. Therefore, firms minimize their loss function, the discounted deviations from p_t^* over all t:

$$\min_{x_t} \left\{ E_t \left[k \sum_{j=0}^{\infty} \beta^j \phi^j \left(x_t - p_{t+j}^* \right)^2 \right] \right\}. \tag{21}$$

The parameter $k > 0$ enters the loss function multiplicatively and indicates all exogenous factors that will influence the costs of not setting the optimal price in each period.[20] The first-order condition is

$$\frac{\partial}{\partial x_t} = E_t \left[2k \sum_{j=0}^{\infty} (\beta\phi)^j (x_t - p_{t+j}^*) \right] = 0. \tag{22}$$

Dividing by $2k$, using the fact that x_t is t-measurable, and expanding the sum gives

$$\sum_{j=0}^{\infty} (\beta\phi)^j x_t - \sum_{j=0}^{\infty} (\beta\phi)^j E_t p_{t+j}^* = 0. \tag{23}$$

[19]See Walsh (2010, 241–242) for the use of level variables in Calvo pricing.

[20]Note that it can also come up as an additive term or any other positive monotonic transformation and does not alter the results.

Excluding x_t from the sum, using the formula for an infinite geometric series, and multiplying by $(1-\beta\phi)$ gives

$$x_t = (1-\beta\phi)\sum_{j=0}^{\infty}(\beta\phi)^j E_t p^*_{t+j}. \tag{24}$$

Again, using t-measurability ($E_t p^*_t = p^*_t$) and excluding the first summand provides a sum from $j=1$ to infinity that can be substituted in a subsequent step:

$$x_t = (1-\beta\phi)\left[\sum_{j=1}^{\infty}(\beta\phi)^j E_t p^*_{t+j} + p^*_t\right]. \tag{25}$$

Furthermore, Eq.(24) can be rewritten for $t+1$ (since firms optimize in each period),

$$E_t x_{t+1} = (1-\beta\phi)\sum_{j=1}^{\infty}(\beta\phi)^{j-1} E_t p^*_{t+j} \tag{26.1}$$

$$\Leftrightarrow \quad \beta\phi E_t x_{t+1} = (1-\beta\phi)\sum_{j=1}^{\infty}(\beta\phi)^j E_t p^*_{t+j}, \tag{26.2}$$

for eliminating the sum in (25):

$$x_t = \beta\phi E_t x_{t+1} + (1-\beta\phi)p^*_t. \tag{27}$$

Inserting (20.2) and (20.3) leads to the expression

$$\frac{p_t - \phi p_{t-1}}{1-\phi} = \beta\phi\frac{E_t p_{t+1} - \phi p_t}{1-\phi} + (1-\beta\phi)p^*_t \tag{28.1}$$

$$\Leftrightarrow \quad p_t - \phi p_{t-1} = \beta\phi(E_t p_{t+1} - \phi p_t) + (1-\phi)(1-\beta\phi)p^*_t, \tag{28.2}$$

that only contains parameters and variants of the variable p. Then, with the definition of (14) and first-order Taylor expansion, the inflation rate π can be expressed through differences of p:

$$\begin{aligned} p_t - p_{t-1} &= \ln P_t - \ln P_{ss} - (\ln P_{t-1} - \ln P_{ss}) = \ln P_t - \ln P_{t-1} \\ &= \ln\left(\frac{P_t}{P_{t-1}}\right) = \ln\left(\frac{P_t - P_{t-1}}{P_{t-1}} + 1\right) = \ln(\pi_t + 1) \approx \pi_t. \end{aligned} \tag{29}$$

In the same way, the conditional expectation value for period $t+1$ can be expressed with

$$E_t p_{t+1} - p_t \approx E_t \pi_{t+1}. \tag{30}$$

Since this approximation is sufficiently exact for small values of π, an equality sign will be used for all following calculations. Now (28.2) can be rearranged to insert approximations (29) and (30):

$$\phi(p_t - p_{t-1}) = \beta\phi(E_t p_{t+1} - \phi p_t) + (1-\phi)(1-\beta\phi)p_t^* - (1-\phi)p_t \tag{31.1}$$

$$\Leftrightarrow \qquad \pi_t = \beta E_t \pi_{t+1} + \frac{(1-\phi)(1-\beta\phi)}{\phi}p_t^* - \frac{1-\phi}{\phi}p_t + \beta(1-\phi)p_t. \tag{31.2}$$

Isolating $(p_t^* - p_t)$ and replacing it with the result from last section, Eq.(19), gives

$$\pi_t = \beta E_t \pi_{t+1} + \frac{\alpha_\gamma(1-\phi)(1-\beta\phi)}{\phi}\widehat{y}_t. \tag{32}$$

Usually[21], in a final step, a summarizing parameter $\kappa > 0$ for all parameters, multiplied with $\widehat{y}_t$, will be defined to end up in the NKPC:

$$\pi_t = \beta E_t \pi_{t+1} + \kappa \widehat{y}_t. \tag{33}$$

Both the expected inflation rate $E_t\pi_{t+1}$ and the GDP growth rate around the steady state $\widehat{y}_t$ (or output gap) have a positive impact on π_t since $\beta, \kappa > 0$. Moreover, the slope of the NKPC (κ), depends on all four parameters ($\beta, \gamma, \varepsilon$, and ϕ) of this section.[22]

So far, households' optimization led to aggregated demand and firms' profit optimization led to aggregated supply. Price rigidity was modeled via Calvo pricing which received the NKPC. In the next section, private households optimize their consumption intertemporally under a budget constraint. This leads to a forward-looking IS curve.

2.3 Forward-Looking IS Curve

The objective is to derive an Euler equation via maximizing utility with a dynamic budget constraint. Initially, it is not necessary to formulate an explicit utility function. On the contrary, the general marginal utility gives a better insight into the intertemporal mechanics. Only one specific assumption will be made, namely not considering money, working hours or any other possible utility-gainer. It solely relies on consumption and thus households maximize their intertemporal discounted utility

$$\max_{C_t} \left\{ E_t \left[\sum_{s=t}^{\infty} \beta^{s-t} U(C_s) \right] \right\}, \tag{34}$$

[21]See e.g. Galí (2015, 63) or Walsh (2010, 338).

[22]See Appendix A.8 for a more detailed analysis of κ. Depending on the exact model, the slope of the NKPC can have a slightly different meaning, e.g. Walsh (2010, 336) with a measure for the firm's real marginal costs instead of the output gap.

under the constraint

$$C_t \cdot P_t + B_{t+1} = W_t + (1 + i_{t-1}) \cdot B_t, \tag{35}$$

where W is the nominal wage and B the amount of bonds. The latter provides the link between two periods.[23] The Lagrangian brings both together:

$$\mathscr{L}(C_t, C_{t+1}, B_{t+1}) = E_t\left[\sum_{s=t}^{\infty} \beta^{s-t} U(C_s) - \lambda_s (C_s P_s + B_{s+1} - W_s - (1 + i_{s-1}) B_s)\right]. \tag{36}$$

Here, the control variable is s, while t always designates the starting period. Let W be exogenous, then the households' first-order conditions[24] are

$$\frac{\partial \mathscr{L}}{\partial C_t} = U'(C_t) - \lambda_t P_t \qquad = 0 \tag{37.1}$$

$$\frac{\partial \mathscr{L}}{\partial C_{t+1}} = \beta E_t[U'(C_{t+1})] - \lambda_{t+1} E_t[P_{t+1}] = 0 \tag{37.2}$$

$$\frac{\partial \mathscr{L}}{\partial B_{t+1}} = -\lambda_t + \lambda_{t+1}(1 + i_t) \qquad = 0. \tag{37.3}$$

Inserting (37.1) and (37.2) in (37.3) yields

$$\frac{\beta E_t[U'(C_{t+1})]}{E_t[P_{t+1}]}(1 + i_t) = \frac{U'(C_t)}{P_t} \Leftrightarrow U'(C_t) = \beta \cdot (1 + i_t) \cdot \frac{P_t}{E_t[P_{t+1}]} E_t[U'(C_{t+1})], \tag{38}$$

the Euler equation, revealing the intertemporal relationship of the marignal utility out of consumption.[25] Marginal utility in period t equals the counterpart in $t+1$, corrected by discount factor, nominal interest rate, and the ratio of current and expected future price level. Assuming i_t rises, marginal utility in t would also rise relative to period $t+1$. Given the diminishing marginal utility property and therefore concavity, consumption will be higher in the future.[26]

[23]Depending on the definition of the interest rate, the period can vary. Here it has been chosen in a way so that the interest from period t enters the Euler condition.

[24]Differentiating with respect to C_{t+1} is possible because of linearity and Fatou's lemma regarding the conditional expectation.

[25]See in Appendix A.10 for more about the mechanics behind intertemporal optimization by an alternative calculation via Dynamic Programming.

[26]Note that present consumption could also increase because of the income effect.

One possible formulation[27] for such a function is $U(C_t) = (1-\sigma)^{-1} \cdot (C_t^{1-\sigma} - 1)$ with $\sigma > 0$ implying $1/\sigma$ as the intertemporal elasticity of substitiution (IES).[28] Substituting this in the Euler equation gives

$$C_t^{-\sigma} = \beta \cdot (1+i_t) \cdot \frac{P_t}{E_t[P_{t+1}]} E_t[C_{t+1}^{-\sigma}], \tag{39}$$

which can be expressed as

$$Y_t^{-\sigma} = \beta \cdot (1+i_t) \cdot \frac{P_t}{E_t[P_{t+1}]} E_t[Y_{t+1}^{-\sigma}], \tag{40}$$

when recalling the market clearing condition $Y = C$. The long-run real interest r enters the equation through β since it equals $1/\beta - 1$.[29] Solving for Y_t results in the typical downward sloping IS relationship with real interest and expectations expressed in level variables or including $E_t\pi_{t+1}$:

$$\begin{aligned} Y_t &= \frac{1}{(1+i_t)^{1/\sigma}} \cdot \left((1+r) \frac{E_t[P_{t+1}]}{P_t} E_t[Y_{t+1}^{\sigma}] \right)^{1/\sigma} \\ &= \frac{1}{(1+i_t)^{1/\sigma}} \cdot \left((1+r)(1+E_t\pi_{t+1}) E_t[Y_{t+1}^{\sigma}] \right)^{1/\sigma}. \end{aligned} \tag{41}$$

To prepare the approximation, Eq.(40) will be rearranged. Treating t-measurable variables as constants for the conditional expectation, assuming[30] $Cov_t[P_{t+1}, Y_{t+1}^{\sigma}] = 0$, and taking logs yields

$$\ln \left(E_t \left[\frac{P_{t+1}}{P_t} \cdot \frac{Y_{t+1}^{\sigma}}{Y_t^{\sigma}} \right] \right) = \ln \left(\beta(1+i_t) \right). \tag{42}$$

[27] In an early study, Pratt (1964, 132–134) examined the different classes of utility functions in the context of risk aversion. See also Kranz (2013, 6–8) for an alternative subdivision into square root, logarithm, exponential, and broken rational functions.

[28] The first study about Euler equations describing intertemporal private consumption came from Hall (1978). The Appendix A.11 shows that $1/\sigma$ is indeed the intertemporal elasticity of substitution with respect to (39) and (40).

[29] The relation follows from the steady state Euler equation or see e.g. the Ramsey–Cass–Koopmans model, where in the utility maximizing steady state, the net marginal product of capital equals $1/\beta - 1$ and therefore $\beta = 1/(1+r)$. See Galí (2015, 132) for a more complex definition of the long-term real interest rate.

[30] Since $E_t[P_{t+1}] \cdot E_t[Y_{t+1}^{\sigma}] = E_t[P_{t+1} \cdot Y_{t+1}^{\sigma}] - Cov_t[P_{t+1}, Y_{t+1}^{\sigma}]$, the values are potentially overestimated. However, the assumption at this point (in contrast to Section 4.1) does not alter the results and is only for clarity. The following linearization eliminates second order moments.

With the help of the exponential function, prices and output can be rewritten in their log deviations:

$$\ln E_t \left[\exp\left(\ln\left(\frac{P_{t+1}}{P_t}\cdot\frac{Y_{t+1}^{\sigma}}{Y_t^{\sigma}}\right)\right)\right] = \ln E_t \left[\exp\left(\ln P_{t+1} - \ln P_t + \sigma(\ln Y_{t+1} - \ln Y_t)\right)\right]$$
$$= \ln E_t \left[\exp\left(p_{t+1} - p_t + \sigma(y_{t+1} - y_t)\right)\right]. \quad (43)$$

The next steps involve approximations of both inflation rate and output gap and also a first-order Taylor expansion of both the exponential and the logarithmic function:

$$\Rightarrow \ln E_t \left[\exp\left(\pi_{t+1} + \sigma(\widehat{y_{t+1}} - \widehat{y_t})\right)\right] \quad (44.1)$$
$$\approx \ln E_t \left[1 + \pi_{t+1} + \sigma(\widehat{y_{t+1}} - \widehat{y_t})\right] = \ln\left(1 + E_t\left[\pi_{t+1} + \sigma(\widehat{y_{t+1}} - \widehat{y_t})\right]\right) \quad (44.2)$$
$$\approx E_t\left[\pi_{t+1} + \sigma(\widehat{y_{t+1}} - \widehat{y_t})\right] = E_t\pi_{t+1} + \sigma E_t\widehat{y_{t+1}} - \sigma\widehat{y_t}. \quad (44.3)$$

Steps (44.2) and (44.3) were to bypass Jensen's inequality[31] since the function's curvature is sufficiently small[32]. Together with the right side of Eq.(42), after expressing β with r, log-linearizing, and rearranging,

$$\widehat{y_t} = E_t\widehat{y_{t+1}} - \frac{1}{\sigma}(i_t - r - E_t\pi_{t+1}) \quad (45)$$

follows, a dynamic IS curve with the output gap instead of the actual GDP. Referring to the original graphical IS relation, the curve shifts to the right if the long-term real interest rate r, the output gap expectations $E_t\widehat{y_{t+1}}$ or the inflation expectations $E_t\pi_{t+1}$ rise. However, the slope will rise and the curve becomes flatter if the intertemporal elasticity of substitution $(1/\sigma)$ rises.

After a dynamic utility optimization that yielded the Euler equation, the result could be approximated to an equation dependend on the nominal interest rate i_t, explaining the output gap $\widehat{y_t}$. Until now, there are two equations describing the economy, a linearized Phillips curve and a linearized forward-looking IS curve. Consequently, the equation system cannot be solved for the three t-measurable variables $\widehat{y_t}$, π_t, and i_t. The next section adds a third equation, originating from a loss function by the central bank that links output gap to inflation rate.

[31]See Jensen (1906, 190–192) that $f(EX) \geq E[f(X)]$ holds for concave functions, i.e. the logarithm. See also Billingsley (1995, 449) that Jensen's inequality still holds for the conditional expected value.

[32]The accuracy is comparable to log-linearization for small growth rates. Moreover, the exactness increases for larger values because of $(\ln(x))'' \rightarrow 0$ for increasing x. However, resulting values will always be underestimated.

2.4 Targeting Rule under Discretion

The central bank takes NKPC and IS curve as given and wants to optimally set the interest rate for period t. There are several ways to proceed and before describing the optimization problem, a short summary introduces the different concepts.

An early discussion on how to model policy decisions can be found in the work by Kydland and Prescott (1977). Also, Givens (2012, 1) provides an excellent overview: "In macroeconomic models that embody rational expectations, optimal monetary policies are separated by a dichotomy known in the literature as commitment and discretion." He further writes about discretion: "Changes in the interest rate are [...] the result of period-by-period reoptimization in which foregoing policy intentions are considered irrelevant for current decision making (Givens 2012, 1)." In contrast, under commitment, the central bank has a mandatory inflation target and is able to affect expectations. However, a discretionary monetary policy is more flexible, since the interest or inflation rate (path) is not fixed. Drawbacks could be credibility problems that arise if the central bank has to readjust the interest rate frequently due to a volatile economy or if it sets the interest rate in big leaps. The latter is rarely seen in practice and the more realistic central bank behavior is referred to as inertia, "[...] a series of small adjustments in the same direction, drawn out over a period of months, rather than through an immediate once-and-for-all response to the new development (Woodford 2003a, 1)."

Because of the far simpler approach, it is more tempting to start with an optimization unter discretion. Therefore, the central bank's targeting rule will be derived by minimizing the discounted loss function over all periods[33]

$$\min_{\pi,\, \widehat{y}} \left\{ E_t \left[\sum_{s=t}^{\infty} \beta^{s-t} \left((\pi_s - \pi^*)^2 + \delta \widehat{y}_s^{\,2} \right) \right] \right\}, \tag{46}$$

under the constraints (33) and (45), the Phillips curve and IS curve respectively. Every difference between the inflation rate and the central bank's target π^* results in a loss. In the first instance, $\pi^* = 0$ as it does not change the essential findings. Also, every output gap leads to a loss but is reduced by a weighting factor δ, normally smaller than one. Squaring ensures that higher deviations yield disproportionately higher losses and the optimized variables will not vanish in the derivatives. Moreover, it makes the loss

[33]The loss function can be derived by a second order approximation of the households' welfare loss, first introduced by Rotemberg and Woodford (1999, 54–61). It can also be found in the textbooks by Galí (2015), Walsh (2010), and Woodford (2003b).

function symmetrical[34]. The Lagrangian has to be differentiated with respect to $\widehat{y}_t$, π_t, and i_t, since the central bank sets the nominal interest rate:

$$\mathscr{L}(\pi_t, \widehat{y}_t, i_t) = E_t\Bigg[\sum_{s=t}^{\infty} \beta^{s-t}\left(\pi_s^2 + \delta \widehat{y}_s{}^2\right) - \chi_s(\pi_s - \beta\pi_{s+1} - \kappa\widehat{y}_s) \\ -\psi_s(\widehat{y}_s - \widehat{y_{s+1}} + \frac{1}{\sigma}(i_s - r - \pi_{s+1}))\Bigg]. \tag{47}$$

First-order conditions:

$$\frac{\partial \mathscr{L}}{\partial \pi_t} = 2\pi_t - \chi_t \qquad = 0 \tag{48.1}$$

$$\frac{\partial \mathscr{L}}{\partial \widehat{y}_t} = 2\delta\widehat{y}_t + \chi_t\kappa - \psi_t = 0 \tag{48.2}$$

$$\frac{\partial \mathscr{L}}{\partial i_t} = -\frac{\psi_t}{\sigma} \qquad = 0. \tag{48.3}$$

From condition (48.3) follows that $\psi_t = 0$, hence the minimized loss will not change if the IS curve shifts, as the central bank can counteract it one by one through resetting the nominal interest rate.[35] Combining (48.1) and (48.2), the standard targeting rule under discretion arises:

$$\delta\widehat{y}_t = -\kappa\pi_t \quad \Leftrightarrow \quad \widehat{y}_t = -\frac{\kappa}{\delta}\pi_t. \tag{49}$$

Although the optimal interest rate is not explicitly given, all relationships between the macroeconomic variables are derived. The process is as follows: the nominal interest rate has an effect on the output gap (IS curve), which in consequence affects the inflation rate (NKPC). Furthermore, Eq.(49), the "leaning against the wind" condition, implies a countercyclical monetary policy, that is, to stabilize prices and eventually contract the economy. The degree of this contraction increases in κ and decreases in δ, the weight on output stabilization. Former President of the EBC, Jean-Claude Trichet, picked this up in one of his speeches[36]: "The leaning against the wind principle describes a tendency to cautiously raise interest rates even beyond the level necessary to maintain price stability over the short to medium term [...]."

Despite these explanations, Eq.(49) could give the impression of the central bank acting too contractive (i.e. hawkish[37]). Every (positive) deviation from the inflation

[34]See Nobay and Peel (2003, 661) for an asymmetric loss function (Linex form) that becomes quadratic in a special case.

[35]Blanchard and Galí (2007) call this "divine coincidence,"the lacking trade-off in the basic NKM, and argue that it comes from the absence of real imperfections. Also, Galí (2015, 129) takes only the NKPC and not the IS curve as a constraint since results will not change.

[36]"Asset price bubbles and monetary policy," 8 June 2005, Singapore.

[37]Note that, on the other hand, an expansive monetary policy is referred to as dovish.

target would end up in negative output gap growth. A target larger than $\pi^* = 0$ could make it more realistic but would not change the basic results.

Finally, (33), (45), and (49) can lead to a forward-looking Taylor type rule when relating the original rule in Taylor (1993, 202) to the previous results. Plugging (49) into (33) gives

$$-\frac{\delta}{\kappa}\widehat{y_t} = \beta E_t\pi_{t+1} + \kappa\widehat{y_t} \tag{50.1}$$

$$\Leftrightarrow \qquad \widehat{y_t} = -\frac{\kappa}{\delta+\kappa^2}\cdot\beta E_t\pi_{t+1}, \tag{50.2}$$

which can be utilized for (45):

$$-\frac{\kappa}{\delta+\kappa^2}\cdot\beta E_t\pi_{t+1} = E_t\widehat{y_{t+1}} - \frac{1}{\sigma}(i_t - r - E_t\pi_{t+1}) \tag{51.1}$$

$$\Leftrightarrow \quad -\left(\frac{\beta\kappa\sigma}{\delta+\kappa^2}\right)E_t\pi_{t+1} = \sigma E_t\widehat{y_{t+1}} - i_t + r + E_t\pi_{t+1} \tag{51.2}$$

$$\Leftrightarrow \qquad i_t = E_t\pi_{t+1} + \sigma E_t\widehat{y_{t+1}} + \left(\frac{\beta\kappa\sigma}{\delta+\kappa^2}\right)E_t\pi_{t+1} + r. \tag{51.3}$$

Eq.(51.3) is quite similar to the original Taylor rule in terms of forward-looking variables.[38] Remembering that for simplicity $\pi^* = 0$, the main difference is the coefficient on the expected output gap that can take values much larger than 0.5. The Taylor principle becomes apparent in the coefficient $(\beta\kappa\sigma)/(\delta+\kappa^2)$, the additional amount the central bank should increase the interest rate after an increase in (expected) inflation.

The findings so far can be viewed as the basic New Keynesian framework. Now, the following section extends the model. By implemeting exogenous cost and demand shocks, for Phillips and IS curve respectively, the NKM becomes stochastic.

[38]See also the postulation of a forward-looking rule by Clarida et al (2000, 150) that takes the same form.

3 Persistent Shocks

Recapitulating Section 2, there are now three equations describing the whole economy:

$$\pi_t = \beta E_t \pi_{t+1} + \kappa \widehat{y_t},$$

$$\widehat{y_t} = E_t \widehat{y_{t+1}} - \frac{1}{\sigma}(i_t - r - E_t \pi_{t+1}),$$

$$\text{and} \quad \pi_t = -\frac{\delta}{\kappa}\widehat{y_t} \quad \Leftrightarrow \quad \widehat{y_t} = -\frac{\kappa}{\delta}\pi_t.$$

Section 3 includes shocks that are following an AR(1) process[39] and examines the resulting equilibrium conditions.

3.1 AR(1) Process

Given the possibility that unforseen events might interrupt the normal economic process (e.g., inventions, cold winters, higher oil prices, wars), stochastic shocks can be added to the existing relationships. Compounding the shock from last period and an error term adds the realistic feature of a certain duration of the event that will dwindle over time:[40]

$$e_t = \mu e_{t-1} + \zeta_t \tag{53.1}$$

$$u_t = \nu u_{t-1} + \eta_t \tag{53.2}$$

The coefficients on the shocks in period $(t-1)$, $\mu, \nu \in \,]0,1[$, declare the percentage impact on shocks in period t. Additional assumptions are normally distributed error terms with an expected value equal to zero, that is, $\zeta_t \sim \mathcal{N}(0, \sigma_e^2)$ and $\eta_t \sim \mathcal{N}(0, \sigma_u^2)$, and also serially uncorrelated error terms, meaning covariances of two different periods have to be zero.[41] Adding Eq.(53.1) to the NKPC, Eq.(33), can be described as a cost shock, a cost-push shock or an inflation shock and adding Eq.(53.2) to the IS curve, Eq.(45),

[39] See Mills (1990, 69–72) for an introduction and some calculation rules.

[40] See Clarida et al (2000, 170) also assuming a stationary AR(1) process in the context of a NKM.

[41] The serially uncorrelated assumption is typically made without comment and helps with some calculation steps. It is questionable how grounded in reality this may be but that goes far beyond the scope of this thesis. However, Section 5 takes up this point again.

indicates a taste shock, a demand shock or fluctuations in the flexible-price equilibrium output level (Walsh 2010, 352):[42]

$$\pi_t = \beta E_t \pi_{t+1} + \kappa \widehat{y_t} + e_t \tag{54.1}$$

$$\widehat{y_t} = E_t \widehat{y_{t+1}} - \frac{1}{\sigma}(i_t - r - E_t \pi_{t+1}) + u_t. \tag{54.2}$$

It is possible to transform shocks e_t and u_t into an infinite sum containing the persistence parameter and all error terms until period t. Expressing e_t through e_{t-2} gives

$$e_t = \mu e_{t-1} + \zeta_t = \mu (\mu e_{t-2} + \zeta_{t-1}) + \zeta_t = \mu^2 e_{t-2} + \mu^1 \zeta_{t-1} + \mu^0 \zeta_{t-0}. \tag{55}$$

After n iterations and finally $n \to \infty$:

$$e_t = \mu^n e_{t-n} + \sum_{k=0}^{n-1} \mu^k \zeta_{t-k} \quad \overset{\lim_{n\to\infty}}{\Longrightarrow} \quad e_t = \sum_{k=0}^{\infty} \mu^k \zeta_{t-k} = \zeta_t + \sum_{k=1}^{\infty} \mu^k \zeta_{t-k} \tag{56}$$

and analogously

$$u_t = \sum_{k=0}^{\infty} \nu^k \eta_{t-k} = \eta_t + \sum_{k=1}^{\infty} \nu^k \eta_{t-k}, \tag{57}$$

that is, the shock in period t can be expressed as the actual stochastic term plus the sum of all past shocks weighted by their impact on period t. Remember that $E_t[e_t] = e_t$, but $E[e_t] = 0$. Thus, taking the conditional expectation would not make the formula redundant.

3.2 Uniqueness of an Equilibrium

The present equations can be described as a system of difference equations to examine the possibility of stable points or more precisely the uniqueness of an equilibrium. In its basic form

$$A_t = M \cdot A_{t+1} + A_0, \tag{58}$$

where A_t is a vector of the endogenous variables in period t, A_{t+1} a vector of the forward-looking variables in period $t+1$, and A_0 everything else that additively enters in the equations (i.e., constants and shocks). M is the matrix of the coefficients on the expectation variables.

The paper by Blanchard and Kahn (1980, 1308) showed that systems solved for the t-measurable variables have an unique equilibrium if and only if the coefficient matrix M

[42] See Galí (2015, 128) for a further discussion of cost shocks, the type that is will be most important throughout the remainder of the thesis.

has all eigenvalues (real and imaginary) strictly inside the unit circle, that is, both real and imaginary parts have to be smaller than one.[43] The intuitive (and simplified) explanation is that the system would otherwise be destabilized and/or jump between different points, similar to the geometric series. Applying this to a 2×2 matrix, consisting of Eq.(54.1) and Eq.(54.2), two conditions can be derived. Appendix A.13 shows its own proof using basic algebra to derive necessary and sufficient conditions for the parameter constellations that imply a unique equilibrium. The conditions are

$$|Det(M)| \qquad\qquad < 1 \tag{59.1}$$

$$\text{and} \quad |Trace(M)| - Det(M) < 1. \tag{59.2}$$

In the following, a general forward-looking Taylor rule is used:

$$i_t = r + \alpha_y E_t\widehat{y_{t+1}} + \alpha_\pi E_t\pi_{t+1}, \tag{60}$$

with $\alpha_y = \sigma$, as in the derived Taylor rule in Eq.(51.3), to keep the focus on the inflation parameter. Together with the stochastic curves, Eq.(54.1) and (54.2), the system of equations can be written in matrix form:[44]

$$\begin{bmatrix} \widehat{y_t} \\ \pi_t \end{bmatrix} = M \cdot \begin{bmatrix} E_t\widehat{y_{t+1}} \\ E_t\pi_{t+1} \end{bmatrix} + \text{Shocks}, \tag{61}$$

where

$$M = \begin{bmatrix} 0 & (1-\alpha_\pi)\sigma^{-1} \\ 0 & \beta + \kappa(1-\alpha_\pi)\sigma^{-1} \end{bmatrix}. \tag{62}$$

The shocks play no role since they enter the equations additively. With matrix M not being full rank, condition (59.1) is always satisfied.[45] Condition (59.2) leads to

$$\left|\beta + \kappa\frac{1-\alpha_\pi}{\sigma}\right| < 1 \tag{63.1}$$

$$\Leftrightarrow \quad \beta + \kappa\frac{1-\alpha_\pi}{\sigma} < 1 \ \wedge \ -\beta - \kappa\frac{1-\alpha_\pi}{\sigma} < 1 \tag{63.2}$$

$$\Leftrightarrow \quad \kappa(1-\alpha_\pi) < (1-\beta)\sigma \ \wedge \ \kappa(1-\alpha_\pi) > -(1+\beta)\sigma \tag{63.3}$$

$$\Leftrightarrow \quad -(1+\beta)\sigma < \kappa(1-\alpha_\pi) < (1-\beta)\sigma. \tag{63.4}$$

[43] In the paper, the systems are solved for the expectation value and the eigenvalues have to be outside the unit circle. But recent literature, such as Galí (2015) or Bullard and Mitra (2002), solve for the t-measurable variables. Also, the rearrangement and the interpretation are simpler. However, results are the same.

[44] See Appendix A.14 for the rearrangement in more detail.

[45] Also, one of the eigenvalues will always be zero.

Since $(1-\beta)$ is close to zero, α_π should be greater than one (the Taylor principle), so that $(1-\alpha_\pi)$ is negative. However, α_π should not be too large, otherwise the left side of inequality (63.4) does not hold. All these requirements can be assumed in the current and following setting. Galí (2015, 108) examines this in a similar way and graphically illustrates the conditions. Bullard and Mitra (2002) explore more feedback rules by the monetary authority. Further conditions and a detailed discussion can be found in Woodford (2003b, 252–276). He also gives a good overview of how expectations can behave. Concerning inflation forecast targeting, Svensson and Woodford (2003) also provide a detailed discussion. They focus on the implications for a stable and unique equilibrium under different circumstances depending on the monetary policy. The basic conclusion is that multiple equilibria are possible if households and the central bank base their expectations on each other. After making sure that a stable equilibrium can be assumed, the next subsection puts everything together and simplifies to one equation. This has the advantage that possible parameter values can be examined more easily.

3.3 Equilibrium Condition

A standard approach is chosen to substitute expectations through forward solving. Inserting the targeting rule (49) into the stochastic NKPC (54.1) yields

$$\pi_t = \beta E_t \pi_{t+1} - \frac{\kappa^2}{\delta}\pi_t + e_t \quad \Leftrightarrow \quad \pi_t = \frac{\beta\delta}{\delta+\kappa^2}E_t\pi_{t+1} + \frac{\delta}{\delta+\kappa^2}e_t. \tag{64}$$

Devising the same formula for $t+1$ and substituting π_{t+1} gives

$$\pi_t = \frac{\beta\delta}{\delta+\kappa^2}E_t\left[\frac{\beta\delta}{\delta+\kappa^2}E_{t+1}[\pi_{t+2}] + \frac{\delta}{\delta+\kappa^2}e_{t+1}\right] + \frac{\delta}{\delta+\kappa^2}e_t. \tag{65}$$

With $E_t[E_{t+n}[\pi]] = E_t[\pi]$ and $E_t[e_{t+n}] = \mu^n e_t$, future expectations and shocks will leave the equation:

$$\pi_t = \left(\frac{\beta\delta}{\delta+\kappa^2}\right)^2 E_t[\pi_{t+2}] + \frac{\beta\delta\mu}{\delta+\kappa^2}\cdot\frac{\delta}{\delta+\kappa^2}e_t + \frac{\delta}{\delta+\kappa^2}e_t. \tag{66}$$

After $(n-1)$ iterations, the equation converts to

$$\pi_t = \left(\frac{\beta\delta}{\delta+\kappa^2}\right)^n E_t[\pi_{t+n}] + \frac{\delta}{\delta+\kappa^2}e_t\sum_{j=0}^{n-1}\left(\frac{\beta\delta\mu}{\delta+\kappa^2}\right)^j. \tag{67}$$

Developing n towards infinity and making use of the formula for the infinite geometric series only leaves parameters and the cost shock:

$$\pi_t = \frac{\delta}{\delta+\kappa^2} e_t \cdot \frac{\delta+\kappa^2}{\delta+\kappa^2-\beta\delta\mu}. \tag{68}$$

Reducing the fraction, factoring out, and setting $\theta = (\kappa^2 + (1-\beta\mu)\delta)^{-1}$ as auxiliary parameter results in the equilibrium conditions[46] for π_t and $\widehat{y_t}$:

$$\pi_t = \frac{\delta}{\kappa^2+(1-\beta\mu)\delta} \cdot e_t \; = \delta\theta e_t \tag{69.1}$$

$$\text{and} \quad \widehat{y_t} = \frac{-\kappa}{\kappa^2+(1-\beta\mu)\delta} \cdot e_t \; = -\kappa\theta e_t. \tag{69.2}$$

Determine the expectation values[47] analogously:

$$E_t\pi_{t+1} = \delta\theta E_t e_{t+1} = \delta\mu\theta e_t \tag{70.1}$$

$$\text{and} \quad E_t\widehat{y_{t+1}} = -\kappa\theta E_t e_{t+1} = -\kappa\mu\theta e_t. \tag{70.2}$$

Solving the IS curve for the target interest rate yields

$$i_t = r - \sigma\widehat{y_t} + \sigma E_t\widehat{y_{t+1}} + E_t\pi_{t+1} + \sigma u_t, \tag{71}$$

which can be rewritten with the equilibrium conditions (69.2), (70.1), and (70.2):

$$i_t = r + \sigma\kappa\theta e_t - \sigma\kappa\mu\theta e_t + \delta\mu\theta e_t + \sigma u_t. \tag{72}$$

Simplifying results in

$$i_t = r + ((1-\mu)\sigma\kappa + \mu\delta)\theta e_t + \sigma u_t \tag{73}$$

and finally setting $\alpha_\mu > 0$ as a summarizing parameter gives

$$i_t = r + \alpha_\mu e_t + \sigma u_t, \tag{74}$$

a reduced-form solution for the nominal interest rate that describes the equilibrium behavior under optimal discretion. The central bank's optimized interest rate in period t can be expressed through the long-run real interest rate and both shocks which are

[46] See also Clarida et al (1999, 1680) for a comparison of these results to those under commitment.

[47] $E_t e_{t+1} = E_t\left[\mu e_t + \zeta_{t+1}\right] = \mu E_t e_t + \underbrace{E_t\zeta_{t+1}}_{=0} = \mu e_t.$

weighted by a composition of parameters. Since these coefficients are postive, larger shocks correspond to higher interest rates.[48]

Galí (2015, 133–134) refers to this equation type as instrument rule. In contrast to targeting rules (see Eq.(49), "practical guides for monetary policy"), Eq.(74) is not easy to implement.[49] It requires real-time observation of variations in the cost-push shock and the knowledge of the model's parameters, including the efficient interest rate r. However, Eq.(74) will be examined in a theoretical way in order to understand how shocks and persistence correspond to i_t in the equilibrium.

Since the equilibrium condition in this subsection is simple enough, it is worth examining the complete Eq.(73) via comparative statics before simulating the results with concrete values.

[48] See also Walsh (2010, 364) for a more detailed discussion.

[49] The paper by Svensson and Woodford (2005) discusses the "targeting" vs. "instrument" topic in more detail.

3.4 Comparative Static Analysis

The coefficient on the cost shock α_μ contains all used parameters but exploring it analytically is still feasible. Remembering

$$\alpha_\mu = \frac{(1-\mu)\sigma\kappa + \mu\delta}{\kappa^2 + (1-\beta\mu)\delta}, \tag{75}$$

the interdependencies of the equilibrium condition (74) can be systematically examined. Differentiating with respect to all parameters (the impact variation of the cost shock on the interest rate) yields:

$$\frac{\partial \alpha_\mu}{\partial \beta} = -\frac{(1-\mu)\sigma\kappa + \mu\delta}{(\kappa^2 + (1-\beta\mu)\delta)^2} \cdot (-\mu\delta) > 0 \tag{76.1}$$

$$\begin{aligned}
\frac{\partial \alpha_\mu}{\partial \delta} &= \frac{\mu\kappa^2 + \mu(1-\beta\mu)\delta - (1-\mu)\sigma\kappa(1-\beta\mu) - \mu\delta(1-\beta\mu)}{(\kappa^2 + (1-\beta\mu)\delta)^2} \\
&= \frac{\mu\kappa^2 - \sigma\kappa + \mu\sigma\kappa + \beta\mu\kappa\sigma - \beta\mu^2\kappa\sigma}{(\kappa^2 + (1-\beta\mu)\delta)^2} = \frac{\kappa\mu\sigma(\frac{\kappa}{\sigma} - \frac{1}{\mu} + 1 + \beta - \beta\mu)}{(\kappa^2 + (1-\beta\mu)\delta)^2} \\
&= \frac{\kappa\mu\sigma(\frac{\kappa}{\sigma} - \frac{1-\mu}{\mu} + \beta(1-\mu))}{(\kappa^2 + (1-\beta\mu)\delta)^2} \lesseqgtr 0
\end{aligned} \tag{76.2}$$

$$\begin{aligned}
\frac{\partial \alpha_\mu}{\partial \kappa} &= \frac{(1-\mu)\sigma\kappa^2 + (1-\mu)\sigma(1-\beta\mu)\delta - (1-\mu)\sigma 2\kappa^2 - \mu\delta 2\kappa}{(\kappa^2 + (1-\beta\mu)\delta)^2} \\
&= \frac{(1-\mu)\sigma \cdot ((1-\beta\mu)\delta - \kappa^2) - \mu\delta 2\kappa}{(\kappa^2 + (1-\beta\mu)\delta)^2} \lesssim 0
\end{aligned} \tag{76.3}$$

$$\begin{aligned}
\frac{\partial \alpha_\mu}{\partial \mu} &= \frac{(\delta - \sigma\kappa)(\kappa^2 + (1-\beta\mu)\delta) - ((1-\mu)\sigma\kappa + \mu\delta)(-\beta\delta)}{(\kappa^2 + (1-\beta\mu)\delta)^2} \\
&= \frac{(\delta - \sigma\kappa)\kappa^2 + (\beta - 1)\sigma\kappa\delta + \delta^2}{(\kappa^2 + (1-\beta\mu)\delta)^2} \lesseqgtr 0
\end{aligned} \tag{76.4}$$

$$\frac{\partial \alpha_\mu}{\partial \sigma} = \frac{(1-\mu)\kappa}{\kappa^2 + (1-\beta\mu)\delta} > 0 \tag{76.5}$$

Derivative (76.1) is strictly postive. The negative impact of β on κ is of no consequence since $\kappa > 0$. Given positive shocks e_t, a higher β increases the relative intertemporal consumption and therefore C_{t+1} increases. This leads to different expectations and also increases $E_t\widehat{y_{t+1}}$. Eq.(51.3), the forward-looking Taylor rule, prompts the central bank to raise the nominal interest rate. As an additional effect, a larger β decreases the long-run interest rate and ensures lower interest rates i_t.

The sign of the derivative (76.2) can be postive or negative. The determining factor can be simplified to $\sigma(1-\frac{1}{\mu}) + \beta(\sigma - \mu) + \kappa$. There is a positive impact with medial values for μ and a negative effect with small and large values. Generally, a negative impact would be expected, that is, a more dovish policy with a flexible inflation target.

Usually, the impact of κ should be slightly negative. Accordingly, a steeper NKPC (inflation reacts more strongly to the output gap) is accompanied by lower interest rates when shocks are positive. The opposite holds true if μ is very small.

The sign of the derivative (76.4) is also ambivalent. A positive impact arises from large values for δ, that is, more persistent and positive cost shocks lead the interest rate to increase. This is a correlation that would be expected. If δ takes small values, the central bank has no desire to stabilize the output gap and the interest rate is positively correlated to more persistent cost shocks.

Finally, the derivative (76.5) is strictly positive. Larger (smaller) IES decreases (increases) the impact of shocks on the interest rate. To be more precise, if σ decreases, relative consumption (tomorrow/today) reacts more strongly to an interest rate increase. That makes it easier to shift consumption from today to tomorrow. The smaller the ability to intertemporally transfer private consumption, the stronger is the impact of a demand shock in the equilibrium since σ is also the coefficient on u_t.

3.5 Parameter Discussion

Eq.(74) already includes all parameters of the model.[50] This subsection gives a brief overview over possible values. In the following sections, these are used to graphically depict the equilibrium conditions.

The discount parameter β is typically close to 1. Galí (2015, 67) and Rotemberg and Woodford (1997, 321) set β equal to 0.99 (quarterly), whereas Jensen (2002, 939) uses this under an annual interpretation. Walsh (2010, 362) also sets it to 0.99. Galí and Gertler (1999, 207) estimate a value of 0.988. A quarterly $\beta = 0.99$ implies a yearly real rate of return $r = 4.1\%$.[51] To keep the framework close to the actual interest setting of the central bank, all calculations are carried out quarterly and β will be set to 0.99 in the baseline (BL) calibration.

The slope of the NKPC κ takes values close to zero and usually lower than 1. Roberts (1995, 982) estimates in his original NKPC article $\kappa \approx 0.3$. On a quarterly basis, Walsh (2010, 362) sets 0.05, Galí and Gertler (1999, 13) estimate 0.02, and McCallum and Nelson (2004, 47) suggest $0.01 - 0.05$. Jensen (2002, 939) calibrates an annual value of 0.142,

[50] Note that variances σ_e^2 and σ_u^2 are only indirectly included. However, σ_e^2 enters the interest equation in Section 4.

[51] $\frac{1}{\beta^4} - 1 = r$.

whereas Clarida et al (2000, 170) set 0.3 (yearly) and give a range of 0.05 to 1.22 in the literature. In the following simulations, κ is set to 0.04[52].

Woodford (2003a, 165) states that a value of 1 is customary in the RBC literature for σ, the multiplicative inverse of the IES (see, e.g. Clarida et al (2000, 170), Galí (2015, 67), Yun (1996, 359)). A slightly larger value (1.5) is set by Jensen (2002, 939), and Smets and Wouters (2002, 40) estimate 1.6. An insightful metadata study by Havranek et al (2015) estimates a mean IES of 0.5 ($\sigma = 2$) across all countries. However, they report that higher developed countries have a higher IES (lower σ). Therefore, σ will be set to 1.

The weight on output fluctuations δ is set to 0.25 in almost all the literature (see, e.g. Walsh (2010, 362), 939), McCallum and Nelson (2004, 47), Jensen (2002, 939)). The latter reports values from 0.05 to 0.33 in other papers. Thus, $\delta = 0.25$ will also be assumend for the primary simulation. However, in an additional strict inflation scenario, at the end of Section 3, $\delta = 0.01$.

Walsh (2003, 275) allows values up to 0.7 for μ, the cost shock persistence. Clarida et al (2000, 170) set 0.27 (yearly) and Galí and Rabanal (2004, 48) estimate 0.95. Generally, Smets and Wouters (2002, 40) estimate persistencies of 0.8 and higher, which can be confirmed by Smets and Wouters (2007, 29) with 0.89. Thus, μ will be treated as a variable in the range of $0.6 - 0.9$. The smallest value 0.6 implies only 0.1296 on an annual basis.

For the standard deviation of a cost shock, Sims (2011, 17) sets 0.01 ($\sigma_e^2 = 0.0001$), Jensen (2002, 939) sets 0.015 ($\sigma_e^2 = 0.000225$), and Galí and Rabanal (2004, 48) estimate 0.011 ($\sigma_e^2 = 0.000121$). McCallum and Nelson (2004, 47) set an annualized standard deviation of 0.02 ($\sigma_e^2 = 0.0004$). The conservative value of 0.0001 will be taken for the simulation.

Subsection 4.3 reveals that the demand shock persistence ν and σ_u^2 are not needed. Nevertheless, Jensen (2002) sets $\nu = 0.3$, Galí (2015, 72) chooses a value of 0.9, and Galí and Rabanal (2004, 48) estimate 0.93. In general, σ_u^2 takes the same values as σ_e^2. However, Galí and Rabanal (2004, 48) estimate it as roughly five times larger.

[52]Note that this implies $\kappa = 0.16$ on a yearly basis.

Table 4 shows the used baseline values and the overall range that is used when taking all simulations into account. Every value is assumed to be obtained on a quarter-yearly basis. In order to cover even extreme scenarios, e_t initially ranges from -0.5% to 2.5%.

Table 4: Overview of all Parameters

Parameter	BL Calibration	Applied Range	Description
β	0.99	0.98 - 0.99	Discount factor
κ	0.04	0.01 - 0.25	Slope of the NKPC
σ	1	0.5 - 10	Reciprocal value of the IES
δ	0.25	0.01 - 0.5	Weight on output fluctuations
μ	0.6 - 0.9	0.6 - 0.9	Cost shock persistence
σ_e^2	0.0001	0.00005 - 0.0005	Cost shock variance
e_t	-0.005 - 0.025	-0.005 - 0.025	Cost shock
u_t	0	-0.01 - 0	Demand shock

3.6 Numerical Simulation

Figure 2 shows a simulation of Eq.(73) with quarterly values for μ reaching from 0.6 to 0.9 and values for e_t reaching from -0.5% to 2.5%. The corresponding interest rate takes values from -3% up to 20.9%.

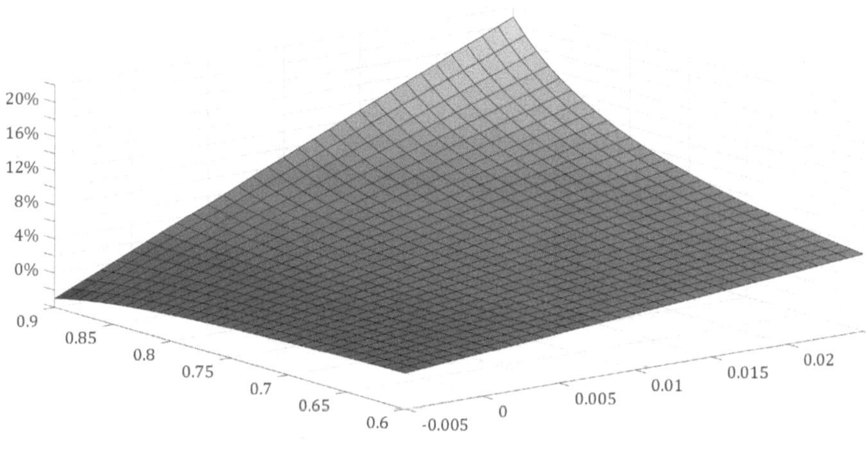

Figure 2: Corresponding interest rate in the equilibrium condition. Horizontal axes: Persistence μ and cost shock e_t. Vertical axis: Interest rate i_t.

It is assumed that negative interest rates are possible and that the zero lower bound does not represent an obstacle. Central banks can indeed raise a tax on deposits made by commercial banks.[53] When the model calibrates negative values for i_t, it could also be interpreted as an unconventional policy (i.e., quantitive easing) by the monetary authorities.[54] The lowest interest rates occur hand in hand with highly persistent negative cost shocks, a fairly extreme scenario since the only major developed country to have faced deflationary tendencies over a prolonged period of time is Japan. But even in this case, the negative cost shocks were closer to zero. As expected, the highest values come with large cost shocks. For a low persistence, regardless of the shocks, the resulting interest rate varies very litte. Overall, there is an average interest rate level of 4.55%. In the last subsection, Table 5 shows for all simulations minimum, maximum, and mean interest values. As a comparison to the uncertainty model in Section 4, Figure 2 will serve as the main reference.

Strict Inflation Targeting

As seen before, Walsh (2010, 362), among others, suggests a value of 0.25 for δ. However, to examine Eq.(74) in a simpler form, δ is chosen to be close to zero.[55] When the central bank utilizes strict inflation targeting, Eq.(73) further shrinks to

$$i_t = r + \frac{(1-\mu)\sigma}{\kappa} e_t + \sigma u_t = r + \sigma\left((1-\mu)\kappa^{-1} e_t + u_t\right), \tag{77}$$

that is, no weight on output stabilization. Furthermore, the "lean against the wind" condition becomes $\pi_t = 0$, meaning that the central bank aims for the inflation target, regardless of the output gap. Although the fraction in Eq.(77) no longer contains the time preference, β still enters the equation through r. Therefore, a larger β corresponds to a smaller i_t. κ behaves in the same way, since a steeper NKPC increases the impact of $\widehat{y}_t$ on π_t and hence the central bank only requires smaller changes in the output gap to influence the inflation. In contrast, a larger σ increases the impact of both shocks on the equilibrium level of the nominal interest rate. This is due to a limited intertemporal elas-

[53] The concise paper by Bassetto (2004) derives a framework in which the central bank commits to negative nominal interest rates and discusses the equilibrium condition in such a situation.

[54] The Wu-Xia shadow rate does exactly that, see Wu and Xia (2014), and was at −3% in May 2014 for the federal funds rate.

[55] When considering Eq.(64), it would be mathematically correct to apply

$$i_t = \lim_{\delta \to 0} (r + \alpha_\mu e_t + \sigma u_t) = r + \lim_{\delta \to 0} \left(\frac{(1-\mu)\sigma\kappa + \mu\delta}{\kappa^2 + (1+\beta\mu)\delta} \right) + \sigma u_t.$$

However, to satisfy the trade-off between simplification and realism, the central bank chooses $\delta = 0.01$, to have the possibility to deviate slightly from the inflation target.

ticity of substitution that dampens the relative consumption's reaction after an increase in i_t. The central bank needs larger changes in i_t to utilize this link. And finally, a more persistent cost shock (larger μ) increases the effect of e_t on i_t. With a larger μ (close to 1), almost the same shock is expected in the next period. An intertemporal shift of demand only postpones the inflation (postive or negative) problem. The central bank is confronted with a trade-off.

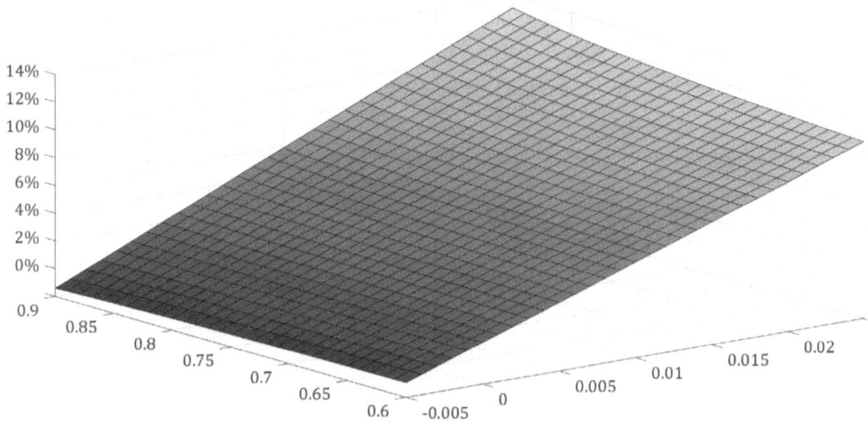

Figure 3: Corresponding interest rate in an equilibrium condition with strict inflation targeting. Horizontal axes: Persistence μ and cost shock e_t. Vertical axis: Interest rate i_t.

Figure 3 shows a simulation with values for μ reaching from 0.6 to 0.9 and values for e_t reaching from -0.5% to 2.5% on a quarterly basis. The corresponding interest rate takes values from marginally below -1.4% up to 13.1%. The straight, upward sloping area shows that persistence has hardly no influence on i_t anymore. Under discretion, persistence does not matter since every period can be optimized independently to attain the inflation target in all t. This is a result that could be worth delving further into if the central bank acts under commitment and is able to affect private expectations. Because the central bank can now reach its goal with more ease, the range of interest rate values shrinks in comparison to Figure 2.

4 Model with Uncertainty

4.1 Quadratic Approximation

Calvo Pricing and the Central Bank's Loss Function. Two out of the three derived equations are already underlain with a quadratic approximation. Variance parameters enter neither the NKPC nor the targeting rule. The next formula will be used to check this for the Calvo pricing objective function and is needed later on as a key step to incorporate the variance in the IS curve. To obtain the second moment, the formula for the conditional variance in terms of the first moments is used. In general:

$$Var_t z_{t+1} = E_t z_{t+1}^2 - (E_t z_{t+1})^2 \Leftrightarrow E_t z_{t+1}^2 = (E_t z_{t+1})^2 + Var_t z_{t+1}. \tag{78}$$

The variance in Calvo Pricing,

$$E_t\left[(x_t - p_{t+j}^*)^2\right] = Var_t[x_t - p_{t+j}^*] + \left(E_t[x_t - p_{t+j}^*]\right)^2 = Var_t[p_{t+j}^*] + \left(x_t - E_t[p_{t+j}^*]\right)^2, \tag{79}$$

vanishes in the first derivative:

$$(..)' = 0 + 2x_t - 2E_t[p_{t+j}^*]. \tag{80}$$

This is due to the t-measurability of the optimizing variable x_t. Furthermore, the loss function can be derived by a second-order approximation of the households' welfare loss, as mentioned earlier. Here, the linearity of the constraint prevents the variance from entering the first-order condition.[56]

The Quadratic IS Curve

The case of uncertainty only differs in the derivation of the IS curve. Eq.(40) can be prepared for quadratic approximation when inserting $1/(1+r)$ for β, rearranging, and taking logs:

$$\ln\left(\frac{1+r}{1+i_t}\right) = \ln E_t\left[\left(\frac{Y_{t+1}}{Y_t}\right)^{-\sigma}\right] - \ln E_t\left[\frac{P_{t+1}}{P_t}\right]. \tag{81}$$

[56]Note that even when the IS curve becomes quadratic, the derivation of the targeting rule stays the same since the shifts through variance are more important than the curvature.

Section 2.3 showed that ignoring Jensen's inequality is equivalent to first-order Taylor series expansions of both logarithm and exponential function. Hence, the right side of Eq.(81) can be written as

$$\gtrapprox E_t \left[\ln \left(\left(\frac{Y_{t+1}}{Y_t} \right)^{-\sigma} \right) \right] - E_t \left[\ln \left(\frac{P_{t+1}}{P_t} \right) \right] \tag{82}$$

and thereby be expressed in growth rates[57]:

$$E_t[-\sigma \ln(1 + \widetilde{y_{t+1}})] - E_t[\ln(1 + \pi_{t+1})]. \tag{83}$$

Instead of linearizing, the logarithm will be represented by a second-degree polynomial[58]:

$$\approx E_t \left[-\sigma \left(\widetilde{y_{t+1}} - \frac{1}{2} \widetilde{y_{t+1}}^2 \right) \right] - E_t \left[\pi_{t+1} - \frac{1}{2} \pi_{t+1}^2 \right] \tag{84.1}$$

$$= -\sigma E_t \widetilde{y_{t+1}} + \frac{\sigma}{2} E_t \widetilde{y_{t+1}}^2 - E_t \pi_{t+1} + \frac{1}{2} E_t \pi_{t+1}^2 \tag{84.2}$$

$$= \sigma \widehat{y_t} - \sigma E_t \widehat{y_{t+1}} + \frac{\sigma}{2} E_t \widetilde{y_{t+1}}^2 - E_t \pi_{t+1} + \frac{1}{2} E_t \pi_{t+1}^2. \tag{84.3}$$

Bringing together the linearized form of the left side in Eq.(81) and rearranging in the same manner as in Section 2.3 yields the quadratic IS curve:

$$\widehat{y_t} = E_t \widehat{y_{t+1}} - \frac{1}{\sigma}(i_t - r - E_t \pi_{t+1}) - \frac{1}{2\sigma} E_t \pi_{t+1}^2 - \frac{1}{2} E_t \widetilde{y_{t+1}}^2. \tag{85}$$

As before, the percentage deviation from the steady state ($\widehat{y_t}$) positively depends on expected output gap, expected inflation, and real interest. The second-order terms have a negative effect on $\widehat{y_t}$. However, Eq.(85) is not in reduced-form since the last term still contains $\widehat{y_t}$. Again, Eq.(78), the formula for the variance, can be utilized to show the second moments' influence in detail:[59]

$$\begin{aligned} \widehat{y_t} =& E_t \widehat{y_{t+1}} - \frac{1}{\sigma}(i_t - r - E_t \pi_{t+1}) - \frac{1}{2\sigma} Var_t \pi_{t+1} - \frac{1}{2} Var_t \widetilde{y_{t+1}} \\ & - \frac{1}{2\sigma}(E_t \pi_{t+1})^2 - \frac{1}{2}(E_t \widetilde{y_{t+1}})^2. \end{aligned} \tag{86}$$

[57]Note that the use of the actual GDP growth rate $\widetilde{y_{t+1}}$ in Eq.(83) is merely for clarity. See Appendix A.6 and in particular Eq.(A10.3) for the relationship between $\widetilde{y_{t+1}}$ and $\widehat{y_{t+1}}$.

[58]See Appendix A.15 for more detail.

[59]Note that $Var_t \widetilde{y_{t+1}} \approx Var_t(\widehat{y_{t+1}} - \widehat{y_t}) = Var_t \widehat{y_{t+1}}$ because $\widehat{y_t}$ is t-measurable and constants (in period t) do not affect Var_t.

In a first step, looking only at the variances and solving for the interest rate yields

$$i_t = -\sigma\widehat{y_t} + r + E_t\pi_{t+1} + \sigma E_t\widehat{y_{t+1}} - \frac{1}{2}Var_t\pi_{t+1} - \frac{\sigma}{2}Var_t\widehat{y_{t+1}} - \dots, \tag{87}$$

which states that uncertainty would shift the curve to the left compared to the former IS curve. Considering the second moment, there are two additional effects, namely expected output gap growth affects the slope and also a variation of the curve's shape. That is because the last term of Eq.(86) contains $\widehat{y_t}$ and $\widehat{y_t}^2$:

$$-\frac{1}{2}(E_t\widehat{y_{t+1}} - \widehat{y_t})^2 = -\frac{1}{2}(E_t\widehat{y_{t+1}})^2 + E_t\widehat{y_{t+1}} \cdot \widehat{y_t} - \frac{1}{2}\widehat{y_t}^2. \tag{88}$$

Inserting everything in Eq.(87) gives

$$\begin{aligned} i_t = &-\frac{\sigma}{2}\widehat{y_t}^2 + (\sigma E_t\widehat{y_{t+1}} - \sigma)\widehat{y_t} + r + E_t\pi_{t+1} + \sigma E_t\widehat{y_{t+1}} - \frac{1}{2}Var_t\pi_{t+1} - \frac{\sigma}{2}Var_t\widehat{y_{t+1}} \\ &- \frac{1}{2}(E_t\pi_{t+1})^2 - \frac{\sigma}{2}(E_t\widehat{y_{t+1}})^2. \end{aligned} \tag{89}$$

Larger values for $E_t\widehat{y_{t+1}}$ result in a (slightly) flatter IS curve and vice versa. Figure 4 illustrates the shift, the different slope, and the quadratic form.

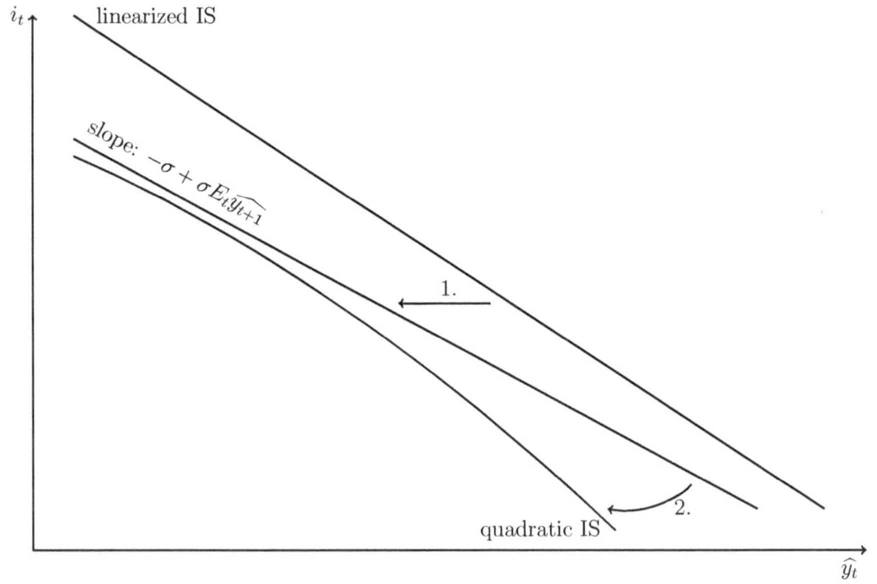

Figure 4: 1. Shift of the locus and a change in the slope (for $E_t\widehat{y_{t+1}} > 0$). 2. The quadratic form.

In the quadratic IS formula, σ is the only parameter besides r. When examining the effects of a variation in σ on the derived curve, it is useful to recapitulate the meaning of $1/\sigma$. The IES measures the strength of the relationship between i_t and $\widehat{y_{t+1}}/\widehat{y_t}$ (also y_{t+1}/y_t and C_{t+1}/C_t). A positive IES implies a positive relationship. Also, if i_t rises, there is a negative effect on $\widehat{y_t}$ due to the substitution effect. If the IES increases (decreases) the relationship gets stronger (weaker) and the IS curve's slope should be flatter (steeper).

Hence, increasing σ should lead to a steeper IS curve. The effect is indeed a more concave and steeper curve. Additionally, it shifts to the left (right) if the uncertainty is relatively high (low) in comparison to the expected values.

The NKPC, the IS curve, and the targeting rule were all derived by second-order approximations. However, this implements uncertainty only in the IS curve since P_{t+1} and Y_{t+1} are non-t-measurable. Thus, besides the IS' quadratic terms, all derivations follow standard approaches.[60]

4.2 Interest Rate Rule with the Quadratic IS Curve

A forward-looking interest rate rule similar the Taylor rule but adding uncertainty (analogously to the end result of Section 2) is obtained when inserting the standard targeting rule in the NKPC[61], solving for $\widehat{y_t}$, and replacing it in the quadratic IS curve:

$$\begin{aligned} i_t =& r + \left(1 + \frac{\beta\kappa\sigma}{\delta+\kappa^2}\right) E_t\pi_{t+1} + \sigma E_t\widehat{y_{t+1}} - \frac{1}{2}Var_t\pi_{t+1} - \frac{\sigma}{2}Var_t\widehat{y_{t+1}} \\ & - \frac{1}{2}(E_t\pi_{t+1})^2 - \frac{\sigma}{2}(E_t\widehat{y_{t+1}} - \widehat{y_t})^2 \qquad (90.1) \\ =& r + \left(1 + \frac{\beta\kappa\sigma}{\delta+\kappa^2}\right) E_t\pi_{t+1} + \sigma E_t\widehat{y_{t+1}} - \frac{1}{2}Var_t\pi_{t+1} - \frac{\sigma}{2}Var_t\widehat{y_{t+1}} \\ & - \left(\frac{1}{2} + \frac{\sigma}{2}\left(\frac{\beta\kappa}{\delta+\kappa^2}\right)^2\right)(E_t\pi_{t+1})^2 - \frac{\sigma}{2}(E_t\widehat{y_{t+1}})^2 - \frac{\beta\kappa\sigma}{\delta+\kappa^2}E_t\pi_{t+1}E_t\widehat{y_{t+1}}. \qquad (90.2) \end{aligned}$$

When examining the coefficients on first and second moments, the parameters β, δ, κ, and σ have to be taken into account. Larger values for β and κ[62] increase the weight on

[60]In addition, an alternative approach regarding the IS curve is imaginable. A quadratic approximation of the exponential function in level variables and then log-linearizing could obtain growth rates. The IS curve would still be linear and the results quite similar except for large interest rates since the accuracy of the approximation decreases. Since this IS curve would include uncertainty but no variances, it could be used for the uniqueness of an equilibrium analysis similar to Section 3.2.

[61]This gives the optimality condition, the output gap expressed in units of expected inflation:

$$\widehat{y_t} = -\frac{\beta\kappa}{\delta+\kappa^2}E_t\pi_{t+1}.$$

[62]The increasing relationship holds for $\delta = 0.25$ (independent of β and σ) if $\kappa < 0.5$, which can be assumed (see Subsection 3.5).

expected inflation, whereas larger values for σ increase the weight on expected inflation, as well as expectation and uncertainty concerning the output gap growth. Following Bauer and Neuenkirch (2015), the squared expected inflation rate, the squared expected output gap growth rate, and their cross product will not be emphasized here, as it takes very small values for advanced economies.

The difference to conventionally derived Taylor rules ultimately lies in the negative variance term that Bauer and Neuenkirch (2015, 15–17) empirically confirmed for uncertainty in future inflation rates where central banks lower the interest rate for higher values of $Var_t \pi_{t+1}$. Branch (2014, 1042–1044) also adds variances in an empirical model and titles it the "nowcasting Taylor rule". He estimates negative coefficients with a more significant (and more negative) value for the coefficient on the inflation variance.

Optimal interest rate for $\pi^* > 0$. When Eq.(47), the Lagrangian attaining the "lean against the wind" condition, is extended with π^* (as in (46), the loss function), the standard targeting rule changes to

$$\pi_t - \pi^* = -\frac{\delta}{\kappa}\widehat{y_t}, \tag{91}$$

whereby the optimal output gap,

$$\widehat{y_t} = -\frac{\beta\kappa}{\delta + \kappa^2} E_t \pi_{t+1} + \frac{\pi^* \kappa}{\delta + \kappa^2}, \tag{92}$$

comprises an additional term. After inserting in the IS curve, the interest rule also has an additional (negative) term. This leads to a generally lower interest level.

Since the corresponding equilibrium condition is going to be more complex, as evident from the next subsection, Section 4 represents the interest rates only numerically.

4.3 Equilibrium Condition

Analogous to Subsection 3.3, an equilibrium condition can be derived through the assumption of stochastic curves following an AR(1) process. The equation system consists of

$$\begin{aligned}
&\pi_t = \beta E_t \pi_{t+1} + \kappa \widehat{y_t} + e_t, \\
&\widehat{y_t} = E_t \widehat{y_{t+1}} - \frac{1}{\sigma}(i_t - r - E_t \pi_{t+1}) - \frac{1}{2\sigma} E_t \pi_{t+1}^2 - \frac{1}{2} E_t \widetilde{y_{t+1}}^2 + u_t, \\
\text{and} \quad &\pi_t = -\frac{\delta}{\kappa}\widehat{y_t} \quad \Leftrightarrow \quad \widehat{y_t} = -\frac{\kappa}{\delta}\pi_t.
\end{aligned}$$

Basically, the approach is solving the IS curve for the interest rate and replacing all variables with shocks. The difference to Section 3 are the quadratic terms, thus lower interest rates should be expected. Furthermore, the next three equations help in unterstanding the subsequent step when inserting the shocks in the squared future inflation and the squared future output gap.

To rearrange the conditional expectation of the squared shocks, formula (78) can be used to obtain the variance and the squared expected value:

$$E_t e_t^2 = Var_t e_t + (E_t e_t)^2 = Var_t e_t + e_t^2. \tag{94}$$

As explained in Subsection 3.1, $E_t e_t = e_t$ and in Eq.(56), e_t can be expressed in past stochastic terms:

$$Var_t \left[\sum_{k=0}^{\infty} \mu^k \zeta_{t-k} \right] + e_t^2 = \sum_{k=0}^{\infty} \mu^k Var_t \left[\zeta_{t-k} \right] + e_t^2 \tag{95}$$

Furthermore, the conditional variance is zero for all periods until t since in period t the volatility is completely pre-determined (deterministic) given previous values. Therefore,

$$E_t e_t^2 = e_t^2. \tag{96}$$

A similar argument can be used to get directly to Eq.(96). The last result helps to replace the IS curve's the second moment terms with shocks in period t. To start with the expected value of the squared inflation ($E_t \pi_{t+1}^2$), Eq.(69.1) in period $t+1$ gives

$$\pi_{t+1} = \delta\theta e_{t+1} = \delta\theta \left(\mu e_t + \zeta_{t+1} \right), \tag{97}$$

by using the former shock definition with persistence and a normally distributed error term. Therefore,

$$E_t \pi_{t+1}^2 = E_t \left[(\delta\theta)^2 \left(\mu e_t + \zeta_{t+1} \right)^2 \right] = (\delta\theta)^2 E_t \left[\mu^2 e_t^2 + 2\mu e_t \zeta_{t+1} + \zeta_{t+1}^2 \right], \tag{98}$$

where the middle term equals zero, since e_t can be treated as a constant in E_t and $E_t \zeta_{t+1} = 0$. Inserting the variance, again with Eq.(78), yields

$$(\delta\theta\mu)^2 e_t^2 + (\delta\theta)^2 \left(Var_t \zeta_{t+1} + (E_t \zeta_{t+1})^2 \right). \tag{99}$$

The variance is defined as σ_e^2 and hence,

$$E_t\pi_{t+1}^2 = (\delta\theta)^2 \left(\mu^2 e_t^2 + \sigma_e^2\right). \tag{100}$$

Doing the same for the expected value of the squared output growth rate[63] ($E_t\widetilde{y_{t+1}}^2 = E_t(\widehat{y_{t+1}} - \widehat{y_t})^2$), Eq.(69.2) in period $t+1$ gives

$$\widehat{y_{t+1}} = -\kappa\theta e_{t+1} = -\kappa\theta\left(\mu e_t + \zeta_{t+1}\right) \tag{101}$$

and therefore,

$$\begin{aligned}
E_t(\widehat{y_{t+1}} - \widehat{y_t})^2 &= E_t\left[\left((-\kappa\theta)\left(\mu e_t + \zeta_{t+1}\right) - (-\kappa\theta)e_t\right)^2\right] && (102.1)\\
&= E_t\left[(-\kappa\theta)^2\left(\mu e_t + \zeta_{t+1} - e_t\right)^2\right] && (102.2)\\
&= (-\kappa\theta)^2 E_t\left[\left((\mu-1)e_t + \zeta_{t+1}\right)^2\right] && (102.3)\\
&= \left((-\kappa\theta)(\mu-1)\right)^2 e_t^2 + (-\kappa\theta)^2\left(Var_t\zeta_{t+1} + (E_t\zeta_{t+1})^2\right) && (102.4)\\
&= \kappa^2\theta^2(\mu-1)^2 e_t^2 + \kappa^2\theta^2\sigma_e^2 && (102.5)\\
&= (\kappa\theta)^2\left((1-\mu)^2 e_t^2 + \sigma_e^2\right). && (102.6)
\end{aligned}$$

The equilibrium condition under uncertainty is now

$$\begin{aligned}
i_t &= r + \alpha_\mu e_t - \frac{1}{2}(\delta\theta)^2\left(\mu^2 e_t^2 + \sigma_e^2\right) - \frac{\sigma}{2}(\kappa\theta)^2\left((1-\mu)^2 e_t^2 + \sigma_e^2\right) + \sigma u_t && (103.1)\\
&= r + \alpha_\mu e_t - \frac{1}{2}\left((\delta\theta)^2\mu^2 e_t^2 + (\delta\theta)^2\sigma_e^2 + \sigma(\kappa\theta)^2(1-\mu)^2 e_t^2 + \sigma(\kappa\theta)^2\sigma_e^2\right) + \sigma u_t && (103.2)\\
&= r + \alpha_\mu e_t - \frac{1}{2}\left(\left((1-\mu)^2\sigma\kappa^2 + \mu^2\delta^2\right)\theta^2 e_t^2 + \left(\sigma\kappa^2 + \delta^2\right)\theta^2\sigma_e^2\right) + \sigma u_t && (103.3)
\end{aligned}$$

and finally setting $\alpha_e > 0$ and $\alpha_\sigma > 0$ as summarizing parameters gives

$$i_t = r + \alpha_\mu e_t - \frac{1}{2}\left(\alpha_e e_t^2 + \alpha_\sigma\sigma_e^2\right) + \sigma u_t, \tag{104}$$

a reduced-form solution for the nominal interest rate that describes the equilibrium behavior under uncertainty.[64] Compared to Section 3, a negative term and an additional

[63] Note that the output gap can also be replaced by the inflation rate with the standard targeting rule (49) to obtain the same results.

[64] Going one step further, e_t and u_t could be replaced by the error terms formula in Equations (56) and (57):

$$i_t = r + \alpha_\mu \sum_{k=0}^{\infty} \mu^k \zeta_{t-k} - \frac{1}{2}\left(\alpha_e\left(\sum_{k=0}^{\infty}\mu^k\zeta_{t-k}\right)^2 + \alpha_\sigma\sigma_e^2\right) + \sigma\sum_{k=0}^{\infty}\nu^k\eta_{t-k}.$$

This visualizes the past (known) shocks that are discounted by μ and ν. Except for the demand shock variance σ_u^2, all introduced parameters are needed to describe the equilibrium.

parameter (σ_e^2) enters the condition. The term entails a generally lower interest rate level. Moreover, a larger cost shock variance also corresponds to lower values for i_t, an essential result.[65]

The next subsection serves as a robustness check and uses a different derivation and approximation to obtain a similar result and compare it to that in Subsection 4.3.

4.4 Further Calculations

In the theoretical part, the paper of Bauer and Neuenkirch (2015) derives the IS curve in a similiar way in order to add uncertainty.[66] In contrast to Section 4.1, they linearize the growth rate first and then add the quadratic terms.

Their quadratic IS curve takes the form of

$$i_t = r - \sigma\widehat{y}_t + \sigma E_t\widehat{y_{t+1}} + E_t\pi_{t+1} - \frac{1}{2}E_t\pi_{t+1}^2 - \frac{\sigma^2}{2}E_t(\widehat{y_{t+1}} - \widehat{y}_t)^2 - \sigma E_t[\pi_{t+1}(\widehat{y_{t+1}} - \widehat{y}_t)], \quad (105)$$

where only the last two terms are different. Again, using Eq.(78) gives

$$-\frac{\sigma^2}{2}Var_t[\widehat{y_{t+1}} - \widehat{y}_t] \underbrace{-\frac{\sigma^2}{2}(E_t[\widehat{y_{t+1}} - \widehat{y}_t])^2}_{\approx 0} - \sigma E_t[\pi_{t+1}\widehat{y_{t+1}}] \underbrace{+\sigma\widehat{y}_t E_t\pi_{t+1}}_{\approx 0}, \quad (106)$$

with the second and fourth term assumed to be close to zero. The third term can be rewritten with Eq.(49) for period $t+1$. Simplifying the variance (t-measurability) and applying the same steps as in Eq.(106) yields

$$-\frac{\sigma^2}{2}Var_t\widehat{y_{t+1}} + \frac{\sigma\kappa}{\delta}E_t\pi_{t+1}^2 \quad (107.1)$$

$$= -\frac{\sigma^2}{2}Var_t\widehat{y_{t+1}} + \frac{\sigma\kappa}{\delta}Var_t\pi_{t+1} + \underbrace{\frac{\sigma\kappa}{\delta}(E_t\pi_{t+1})^2}_{\approx 0}. \quad (107.2)$$

Thus, the overall uncertainty is

$$\left(\frac{\sigma\kappa}{\delta} - \frac{1}{2}\right)Var_t\pi_{t+1} - \frac{\sigma^2}{2}Var_t\widehat{y_{t+1}}. \quad (108)$$

[65] The equation in its static form does not directly contain ν and σ_u^2. This is due to the simplified targeting rule and the resulting assumption that $\widehat{y}$ and π can be represented only through cost shocks.

[66] Appendix A.16 derives it step-by-step.

After inserting the shocks for π_{t+1} and $\widehat{y_{t+1}}$, the difference to Eq.(104) appears:

$$\left(\frac{\sigma\kappa}{\delta}-\frac{1}{2}\right)Var_t[\delta\theta\left(\mu e_t+\zeta_{t+1}\right)]-\frac{\sigma^2}{2}Var_t[-\kappa\theta\left(\mu e_t+\zeta_{t+1}\right)] \tag{109.1}$$

$$=\left(\frac{\sigma\kappa}{\delta}-\frac{1}{2}\right)(\delta\theta)^2\sigma_e^2-\frac{\sigma^2}{2}(\kappa\theta)^2\sigma_e^2 \tag{109.2}$$

$$=-\frac{1}{2}\theta^2\sigma_e^2\left(\left(1-\frac{2\sigma\kappa}{\delta}\right)\delta^2+(\sigma\kappa)^2\right) \tag{109.3}$$

$$=-\frac{1}{2}\theta^2\sigma_e^2\left(\delta^2-2\sigma\kappa\delta+(\sigma\kappa)^2\right) \tag{109.4}$$

$$=-\frac{1}{2}\theta^2\sigma_e^2(\delta-\sigma\kappa)^2. \tag{109.5}$$

When comparing to Eq.(104), the e_t^2-term vanishes (i.e., generally slightly higher interest rates) and the impact of the uncertainty can in fact become zero if $\delta=\sigma\kappa$. But this could only happen in case of a relatively low δ (strict inflation targeting), a relatively high σ (a low IES), and a relatively high κ (steep NKPC). A central bank that persues strict inflation targeting is more likely to leave uncertainty out of consideration since it only has one objective that is easier to reach. In countries with a low IES, the relative consumption hardly reacts to the interest rate. There are less leeway to counterbalance uncertainty with a lower i_t. Through a steep NKPC, the inflation rate reacts heavily to changes in the output. With this connection now being strong enough, it could crowd out the effect of uncertainty.

The remainder shows the results graphically and compare them to Section 3.

4.5 Numerical Simulation

In the baseline calibration, as shown in Table 4, $\beta=0.99$, $\kappa=0.04$, $\sigma=1$, $\delta=0.25$, $\sigma_e^2=0.0001$, μ reaches from 0.6 to 0.9 and e_t from -0.5% to 2%. Since ν and σ_u^2 play no role, when the central bank acts under discretion, u_t is assumed to be zero. The optimal interest rate would react one-to-one and there would be no gain of further insights. However, this assumption is relaxed in the final subsection.

Figure 5 shows the results for the model with uncertainty with a variety of persistence and cost shock combinations. The interest takes values from -3.4% to 18.6%. The area of interest rate values takes the same shape as in Section 3, only i_t is overall smaller when accounting for uncertainty. As Table 5 at the end of this section shows, the mean interest rate is roughly a quarter of a percentage point (or 25 basis points) smaller when comparing to Figure 2, the case without uncertainty.

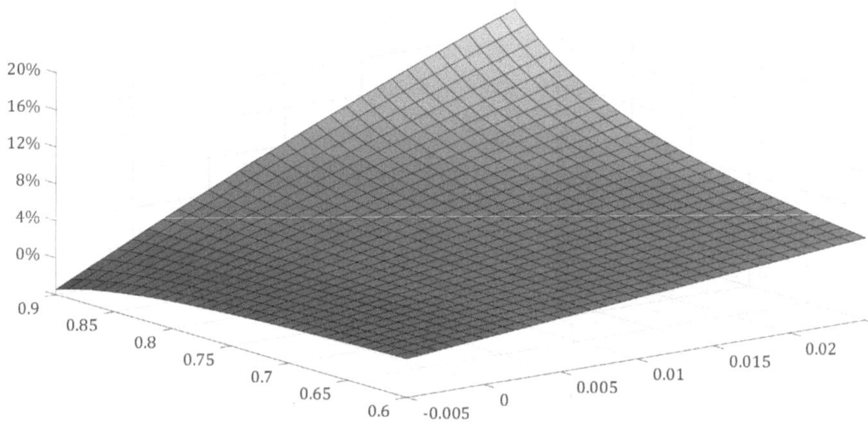

Figure 5: Corresponding interest rate in the equilibrium condition. Horizontal axes: Persistence μ and cost shock e_t. Vertical axis: Interest rate i_t.

In the following, there are two cases being considered that both simplify the equilibrium condition: Strict inflation targeting and the absence of persistent shocks. The former will also be compared to the results in Section 3. Both represent slightly special and unrealistic circumstances but can help to understand how Eq.(104) works.

Strict Inflation Targeting

Eq.(104) simplifies to

$$i_t = r + \frac{(1-\mu)\sigma}{\kappa} e_t - \frac{1}{2}\left(\frac{(1-\mu)^2\sigma}{\kappa^2} e_t^2 + \frac{\sigma}{\kappa^2}\sigma_e^2\right) + \sigma u_t. \tag{110}$$

The equation works in the same way as Eq.(77), only that the values for i_t are slightly lower. Figure 6 reveals the same interest rate pattern since the depicted area looks much as before. There is still a very small δ of 0.01 used in this simulation. Obviously, uncertainty has no influence on the shape.[67] There is an additional squared μ in the formula but the impact of the squared shock is insignificantly small. The values are reaching from -2.6% to 11.5% and the range has roughly the same expanse.

[67]However, there is an interest rate difference of over a half of a percentage point. Appendix A.17 shows this in another figure.

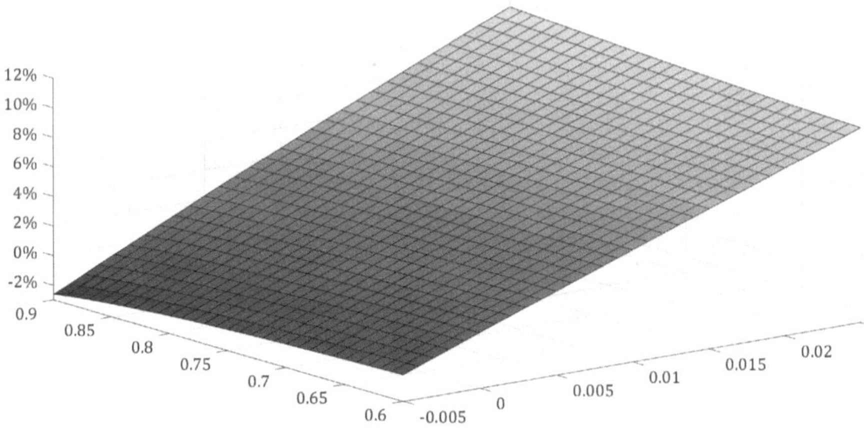

Figure 6: Corresponding interest rate in an equilibrium condition with strict inflation targeting. Horizontal axes: Persistence μ and cost shock e_t. Vertical axis: Interest rate i_t.

No Persistence

There are several changes that occur when the absence of persistent shocks is assumed. First, Eq.(104) simplifies to

$$i_t = r + \frac{\sigma\kappa}{\kappa^2+\delta}e_t - \frac{1}{2}\left(\frac{\sigma\kappa^2}{(\kappa^2+\delta)^2}e_t^2 + \frac{\sigma\kappa^2+\delta^2}{(\kappa^2+\delta)^2}\sigma_e^2\right) + \sigma u_t. \tag{111}$$

Secondly, if the central bank can be sure that a shock only affects one period, generally lower interest rates should be expected. Indeed, in Eq.(111), a coefficient smaller than one $(1-\beta\mu)$ vanishes from the denominators. Squaring even hightens the effect. Finally, κ is now used on one of the horizontal axes since μ is assumed to be zero.

The values for κ in Figure 7 are reaching from 0.01 to 0.1. This results in interest rates from 0.8% to 2%. A very flat NKPC counterbalances the effect of the shock and i_t only depends on the structural parameters. If $\widehat{y_t}$ and π_t do not interact, the central bank can implement a policy more easily and does not need to vary the interest rate to a great extent. A steep NKPC on the other hand allows to use the monetary transmission mechanism to have an additional effect on inflation through output. Another simulation in Appendix A.17 shows that uncertainty plays no role under any level of κ.

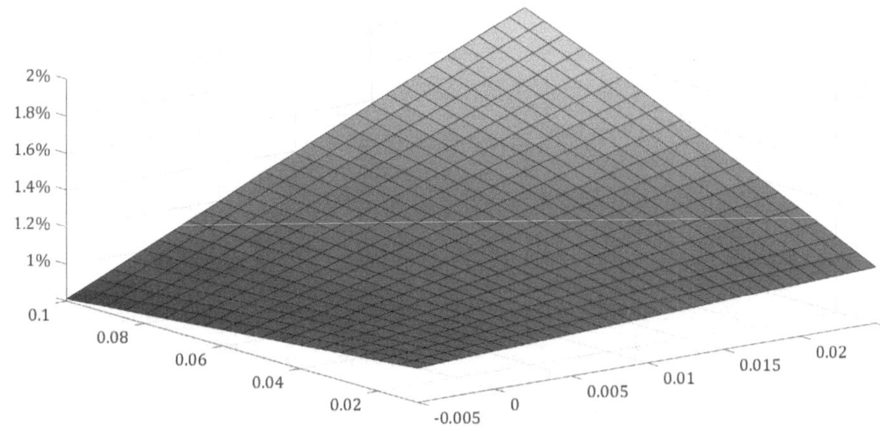

Figure 7: Corresponding interest rate in an equilibrium condition without persistence. Horizontal axes: NKPC's slope κ and cost shock e_t. Vertical axis: Interest rate i_t.

4.6 Model Comparison

In a final step, the results of Section 3 and Section 4 are going to be compared to each other. As mentioned before, relative values play an important role to evaluate the derived model framework in certain settings. Therefore, to isolate the partial effect of the parameters, the interest rate differences after subtracting the values with and without uncertainty are shown under several scenarios. Before the conclusion, the thesis gives an overview over all numerical simulations. Due to small interest rate differences, the vertical axis in the following diagrams is scaled in basis points (100 basis points = one percentage point). Also, basis points as a measure unit play an important role, seeing as one step in the central bank's policy rate corresponds to 25 basis points.

Figure 8 gives a broad overview on the effect of uncertainty. There is a significant amount of persistent/shock combinations that support the estimations by Bauer and Neuenkirch (2015). Especially highly persistent shocks affect the interest rate outcome in the equilibrium behavior. In this case, the interest rate difference reaches from 50 to over 200 basis points. On average, the difference amounts to 24 basis point.

Figure 9 can be understood as a cross section of Figure 8 with $\mu = 0.8$, a realistic assumption when reviewing the literature such as Smets and Wouters (2002). It reveals, as one of the main findings from a theoretical point of view, that accounting for uncertainty results in lower policy rates, even during tranquil times. A black line is drawn at 25 basis points to show the empirical conclusion by Bauer and Neuenkirch (2015, 21).[68]

[68]Note that Bauer and Neuenkirch (2015) have no assumption regarding the level of shock persistence.

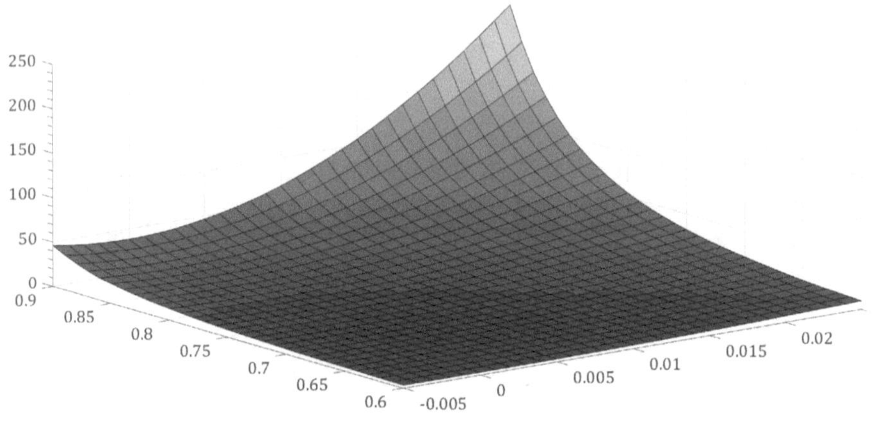

Figure 8: Differences between both cases (with and without uncertainty) in the equilibrium condition. Horizontal axes: Persistence μ and cost shock e_t. Vertical axis: Difference of interest rate i_t in basis points.

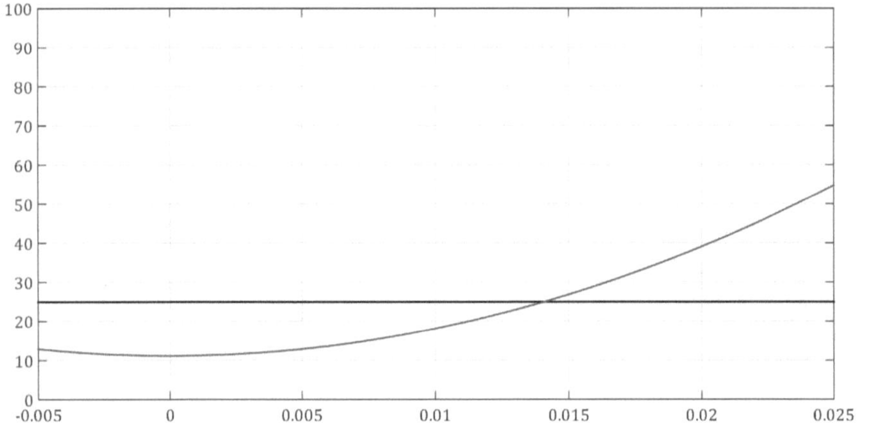

Figure 9: Differences between both cases (with and without uncertainty) in the equilibrium condition ($\mu = 0.8$). Horizontal axis: Cost shock e_t. Vertical axis: Difference of interest rate i_t in basis points.

Scenarios

To give a broader overview but also to see the impact of the parameters in more detail, several scenarios are included in one graph. This makes it easier to compare them to each other. Differences in the interest rate, noted in basis points, are still used. Due to cost shocks and their persistence having been reviewed thoroughly, there is also a wide range of κ values shown in Figure 11. Against this background, it is possible to point out the implications of uncertainty in a particular constellation. In the following two figures, two baseline cases are chosen: a boom ($\beta = 0.98$, $e_t = 1\%$, $\kappa = 0.04$, $\sigma = 1$, $\delta = 0.25$, and $\sigma_e^2 = 0.0001$) and a crisis ($e_t = -0.1\%$, $u_t = -1\%$, $\beta = 0.99$, $\kappa = 0.04$, $\sigma = 1$, $\delta = 0.25$, and $\sigma_e^2 = 0.0001$) scenario. A low β of 0.98 corresponds to yearly returns of over 8% and hence indicates a fast growing economy. Additionally, a moderate cost shock of 1% is considered. On the other hand, a negative demand shock and a small negative cost shock of -0.1% are assumed to take place in a more recessionary state of the economy. Nevertheless, designations and values are chosen freely.

Figure 10 can be understood as a counterpart and also an extended version of Figure 9. The cost shock is now fixed and μ is variable. The black line shows the baseline simulation, dashed shows a κ of 0.2, dotted a σ of 10,[69] and the circle line a σ_e^2 of 0.0002. The diamond line stands for the normal crisis scenario, and triangle and asterisk set κ and σ exactly as in the boom scenarios. High values for κ (triangle and dashed) show almost no differences. A higher variance (circle) has the strongest impact. A very low IES in the third crisis case generally leads to a higher difference, not only for large μ.

Figure 11 is very similar to the preceeding figure. The NKPC's slope is now variable to see the effect of κ on the interest rate behavior. The persistence is now $\mu = 0.9$ as a baseline with the assumption that more extreme scenarios have a more enduring impact. The line scheme slightly differs in some points: black is again the baseline boom scenario, dashed uses a low μ of 0.6, dotted and circle stay the same with $\sigma = 10$ and $\sigma_e^2 = 0.0002$ respectively. Again, the rest of the lines are crisis scenarios. The case of a very low σ is omitted since it does not significantly differ from the baseline case. The influence of uncertainty generally decreases trough a higher κ. As before, high variances show the largest impact and very low intertemporal elasticities have a more continuous effect. A low persistence plays no role.

[69]Havranek et al (2015, 100) suggest values of between 0.1 and 1.5 for the IES. A lower IES tends to be found in emerging markets.

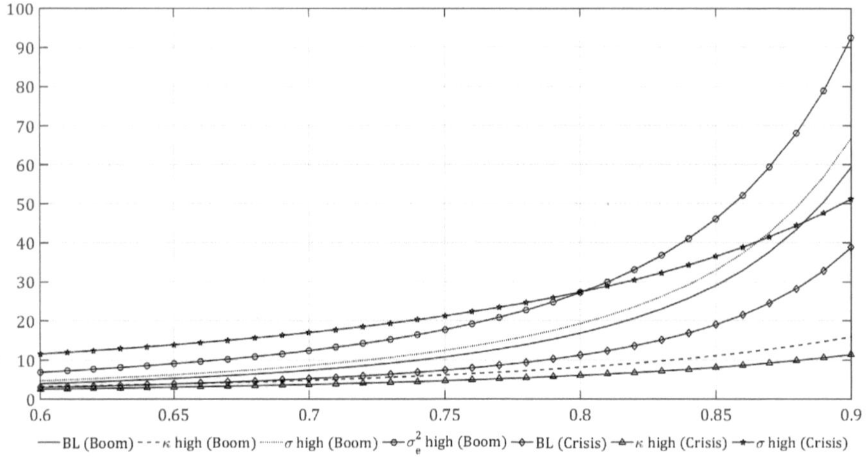

Figure 10: Differences of i_t in several scenarios when μ is variable. Horizontal axis: Cost shock persistence μ. Vertical axis: Difference of interest rate i_t in basis points.

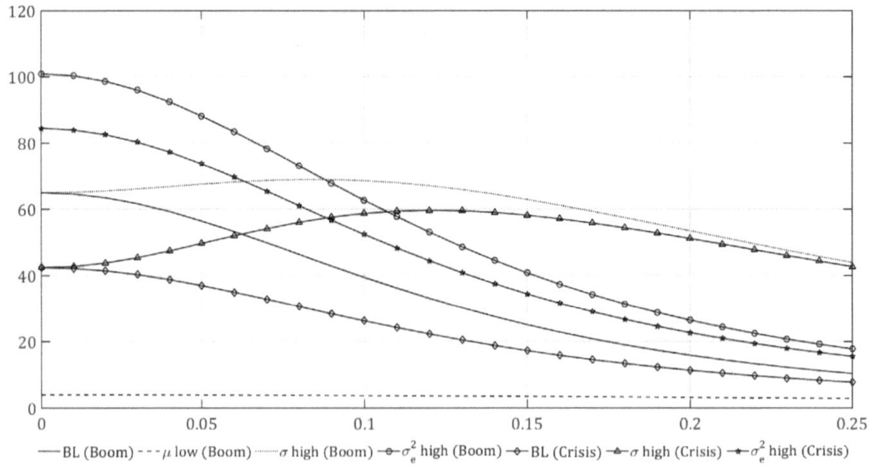

Figure 11: Differences of i_t in several scenarios when κ is variable. Horizontal axis: NKPC's slope κ. Vertical axis: Difference of interest rate i_t in basis points.

Appendix A.18 adds scenarios for a variety of intertemporal elasticties of substitution, weights on output fluctuations, and cost shock variances.[70]

Overview

All numerical simulations (from Section 3, Section 4, and from Appendix A.17 and A.18) are listed in Table 5.

Table 5: Overview of all Simulations

Figure	Section	Description	Min i_t	Max i_t	Mean i_t
2	3.6	Equilibrium Condition	-3%	20.9%	4.55%
3	3.6	Strict Inflation Targeting	-1.4%	13.1%	5.26%
5	4.5	Equilibrium Condition	-3.4%	18.6%	4.31%
6	4.5	Strict Inflation Targeting	-2.6%	11.5%	4.61%
7	4.5	No Persistence	-0.8%	2%	1.22%
8	4.6	Equilibrium Condition Difference	3	229	24
9	4.6	Equilibrium Condition Diff. ($\mu = 0.8$)	11	55	24
10	4.6	Different Scenarios, μ variable	5	48	16
11	4.6	Different Scenarios, κ variable	20	61	40
A4	A.17	Strict Inflation Targeting Difference	27	159	65
A5	A.17	No Persistence Difference	0.5	1	0.6
A6	A.18	Different Scenarios, σ variable	49	69	59
A7	A.18	Different Scenarios, δ variable	46	237	55
A8	A.18	Different Scenarios, σ_e^2 variable	41	228	135

Minimum, maximum, and arthmetic mean are specified in each row. The percentage values of models from Section 3.6 and 4.5 have been rounded to the next decimal place. All other figures involve both models, and values are expressed in basis points, rounded to the next full basis point. The latter holds true in every case exept when the difference without persistence is practically zero and therefore the first decimal place is taken into account. Considering several scenarios, the mean is used to give the values in the last three columns.

[70]Due to the small range of β values, no own diagram is used. However, the typical levels are considered in the graphics.

The table shows that only a small bandwidth of interest rate levels and differences occur even with a wide range of parameter values. Finally, calibrating this general equilibrium model was relatively simple and the result was straightforward: Accounting for uncertainty under average and highly persistent shocks in a New Keynesian model helps to represent the economy in a more realistic way.

5 Conclusion

First, the thesis derived a reduced-form solution for the nominal rate of interest out of a three-equation New Keynesian model with persistent stochastic shocks. Since these shocks behave like an AR(1) process and the central bank's standard targeting rule is applied, this equation describes the equilibrium behavior of the nominal interest rate under optimal discretion. Secondly, this equilibrium was simulated with the focus on persistence parameters. In a next step, the extended model with a quadratically approximated IS curve (therefore with uncertainty) was examined in the same way and compared to the model containing the certainty equivalence. The results give important insights into how the equilibrium behaves when confronted with a wide range of parameter values including possible boom and crisis scenarios:

(i) Interest rates take realistic values and can be interpreted even with a wide range of parameter values. (ii) Interest rates are generally lower when accounting for uncertainty. (iii) This difference increases with higher persistencies and higher cost shocks (positive or negative). (iv) The results are the same with strict inflation targeting in terms of differences but the persistence hardly has any impact on the interest rate behavior. (v) A steeper NKPC decreases the effect of uncertainty. (vi) Finally, and most importantly, the essential result of Bauer and Neuenkirch (2015) can be confirmed from a theoretical point of view. Under sensible assumptions, accounting for uncertainty leads to lower interest rates of roughly 25 basis points. Nevertheless, the outcomes of the numerical simulations are rather indeterminate since no actual interest setting behavior of the central bank was considered.

In an environment with low persistence, uncertainty hardly plays a role because the central bank is assumed to counteract all shocks instantly. Therefore, a targeting rule derived under commitment should be taken into account in order to be further built upon. Due to the negative interest rate in the equilibrium and because of the more prominent role of unconventional monetary policy in recent years, the model could include a zero lower bound while incorporating this kind of policy. Calibrating the shock variance and the underlying distribution, which is essential for the resulting uncertainty, can also be considered as a topic for further research.

References

Akerlof, G. A. and Yellen, J. L. (1985): "A Near-Rational Model of the Business Cycle, With Wage and Price Inertia," *The Quarterly Journal of Economics* 100, 823–838.

Ascari, G. and Rossi, L. (2008): "Long-run Phillips Curve and Disinflation Dynamics: Calvo vs. Rotemberg Price Setting," *Quaderni dell'Istituto di Economia e Finanza* 82-08, Dipartimenti e Istituti di Scienze Economiche, Università Cattolica del Sacro Cuore.

Bassetto, M. (2004): "Negative Nominal Interest Rates," *The American Economic Review* 94, 104–108.

Bauer, C. and Neuenkirch, M. (2015): "Forcasting Uncertainty and the Taylor Rule," *Research Papers in Economics* 05-15, Department of Economics, University of Trier.

Bellman, R. (1957): "A Markovian Decision Process," *Rand Corp* 1066, Santa Monica, CA.

Billingsley, P. (1995): "Probability and Measure," 3rd Edition, Jon Wiley & Sons, New York.

Blanchard, O. J. and Galí, J. (2007): "Real Wage Rigidities and the New Keynesian Model," *Journal of Money, Credit and Banking* 39, 35–65.

Blanchard, O. J. and Kahn, C. M. (1980): "The Solution of Linear Difference Models under Rational Expectations," *Econometrica* 48, 1305–1311.

Blanchard, O. J. and Kiyotaki, N. (1987): "Monopolistic Competition and the Effects of Aggregate Demand," *The American Economic Review* 77, 647–666.

Branch, W. A. (2014): "Nowcasting and the Taylor Rule," *Journal of Money, Credit and Banking* 46, 1035–1055.

Bullard, J. and Mitra, K. (2002): "Learning about Monetary Policy Rules," *Journal of Monetary Economics* 49, 1105–1129.

Calvo, G. A. (1983): "Staggered Prices in a Utility-Maximizing Framework," *Journal of Monetary Economics* 12, 383–398.

Chiang, A. C. and Wainwright, K. (2005): "Fundamental Methods of Mathematical Economics," 4th Edition, McGraw-Hill, New York.

Christiano, L. J., Eichenbaum, M., and Evans, C. L. (2005): "Nominal Rigidities and the Dynamic Effects of a Shock to Monetary Policy," *Journal of Political Economy* 113, 1–45.

Clarida, R., Galí, J., and Gertler, M. (1999): "The Science of Monetary Policy: A New Keynesian Perspective," *Journal of Economic Literature* 37, 1661–1707.

Clarida, R., Galí, J., and Gertler, M. (2000): "Monetary Policy Rules and Macroeconomic Stability: Evidence and Some Theory," *Quarterly Journal of Economics* 105, 147–180.

Dixit, A. K. and Stiglitz, J. E. (1977): "Monopolistic Competition and Optimum Product Diversity," *The American Economic Review* 67, 297–308.

Galí, J. (2015): "Monetary Policy, Inflation, and the Business Cycle," 2nd Edition, Princeton University Press, Princeton, NJ.

Galí, J. and Gertler, M. (1999): "Inflation Dynamics: A Structural Econometric Analysis," *Journal of Monetary Economics* 44, 195–222.

Galí, J. and Rabanal, P. (2004): "Technology Shocks and Aggregate Fluctuations: How Well Does the Real Business Cycle Model Fit Postwar U.S. Data?," *NBER Macroeconomics Annual* 19, 225–288.

Givens, G. E. (2012): "Estimating Central Bank Preferences under Commitment and Discretion," *Journal of Money, Credit and Banking* 44, 1033–1066.

Goodfried, M. and King, R. (1997): "The New Neoclassical Synthesis and the Role of Monetary Policy," *NBER Macroeconomics Annual* 12, 231–296.

Hall, R. E. (1978): "Stochastic Implications of the Life Cycle-Permanent Income Hypothesis: Theory and Evidence," *Journal of Political Economy* 86, 971–987.

Havranek, T., Horvath, R., Irsova, Z., and Rusnak, M. (2015): "Cross-Country Heterogeneity in Intertemporal Substitution," *Journal of International Economics* 96, 100–118.

Jensen, J. L. W. V. (1906): "Sur les Fonctions Convexes et les Inégalités Entre les Valeurs Moyennes," *Acta Mathematica* 30, 176–193.

Jensen, H. (2002): "Targeting Nominal Income Growth or Inflation?," *The American Economic Review* 92, 928–956.

Judd, K. L. (1998): "Numerical Methods in Economics," MIT Press, Cambridge, MA.

Kranz, T. (2013): "Mathematische Grundlagen in Modellen der Ressourcenökonomik: Hydraulic Fracturing und das Cake-Eating-Problem," *Bachelor Thesis*, Department of Economics, University of Trier.

Kydland, F. E. and Prescott, E. C. (1977): "Rules Rather than Discretion: The Inconsistency of Optimal Plans," *Journal of Political Economics* 85, 473–492.

Kydland, F. E. and Prescott, E. C. (1982): "Time to Build and Aggregate Fluctuations," *Econometrica* 50, 1345–1370.

Kyer, B. L. and Maggs, G. E. (1992): "On the Keynes and Pigou Effects in Aggregate Demand Theory," *Journal of Macroeconomics* 14, 371–375.

Lucas, R. E. (1976): "Econometric Policy Evaluation: A Critique," *Carnegie-Rochester Conference Series on Public Policy* 1, 19–46.

Mankiw, N. G. (1985): "Small Menu Costs and Large Business Cycles: A Macroeconomic Model of Monopoly," *The Quarterly Journal of Economics* 100, 529–539.

McCallum, B. T. and Nelson, E. (2004): "Timeless Perspective vs. Discretionary Monetary Policy in Forward-Looking Models," *Federal Reserve Bank of St. Louis Review* 86, 43–56.

Mills, T. C. (1990): "Time Series Techniques for Economists," Cambridge University Press, New York.

Nobay, A. R. and Peel, D. A. (2003): "Optimal Discretionary Monetary Policy in a Model with Asymmetric Central Bank Preferences," *The Economic Journal* 113, 657–665.

Pratt, J. W. (1964): "Risk Aversion in the Small and in the Large," *Econometrica* 32, 122–136.

Prescott, E. C. (1986): "Theory Ahead of Business Cycle Measurement," *Carnegie-Rochester Conference Series on Public Policy* 25, 11–44.

Roberts, J. M. (1995): "New Keynesian Economics and the Phillips Curve," *Journal of Money, Credit and Banking* 27, 975–984.

Roberts, J. M. (1997): "Is Inflation Sticky?," *Journal of Monetary Economics* 39, 173–196.

Romer, D. (2012): "Advanced Macroeconomics," 4th Edition, McGraw-Hill, New York.

Rotemberg, J. J. (1982): "Sticky Prices in the United States," *Journal of Political Economy* 90, 1187–1211.

Rotemberg, J. J. and Woodford, M. (1997): "An Optimization-Based Econometric Framework for the Evaluation of Monetary Policy," *NBER Macroeconomics Annual* 12, 297–361.

Rotemberg, J. J. and Woodford, M. (1999): "Interest Rules in an Estimated Sticky Price Model," in J. B. Taylor (ed), *Monetary Policy Rules*, 57–119, University of Chicago Press, Chicago.

Sims, E. (2011): "Notes on Medium Scale DSGE Models," *Graduate Macro Theory II*, University of Notre Dame.

Smets, F. and Wouters, R. (2002): "An Estimated Dynamic Stochastic General Equilibrium Model of the Euro Area," *ECB Working Paper Series* 171, 1–69.

Smets, F. and Wouters, R. (2007): "Shocks and Frictions in US Business Cycles: A Bayesian DSGE Approach," *NBB Working Paper Series* 109, 1–52.

Svensson, L. E. O. and Woodford, M. (2003): "Indicator Variables for Optimal Policy," *Journal of Monetary Economics* 50, 691–720.

Svensson, L. E. O. and Woodford, M. (2005): "Implementing Optimal Policy through Inflation-Forecast Targeting," in B. S. Bernanke and M. Woodford (eds), *The Inflation-Targeting Debate*, 19–83, University of Chicago Press, Chicago.

Taylor, J. B. (1993): "Discretion versus Policy Rules in Practice," *Carnegie-Rochester Conference Series on Public Policy* 39, 195–214.

Taylor, J. B. (1999): "Staggered Price and Wage Setting in Macroeconomics," in J. B. Taylor and M. Woodford (eds), *Handbook of Macroeconomics*, 1009–1050, Elsevier, New York.

Uhlig, H. (1999): "A Toolkit for Analysing Nonlinear Dynamic Stochastic Models Easily," in R. Marimon and A. Scott (eds), *Computational Methods for the Study of Dynamic Economics*, 30–61, Oxford University Press, New York.

Walsh, C. E. (2003): "Speed Limit Policies: The Output Gap and Optimal Monetary Policy," *The American Economic Review* 93, 265–278.

Walsh, C. E. (2010): "Monetary Policy and Theory," 3rd Edition, MIT Press, Cambridge, MA.

Woodford, M. (2003a): "Optimal Interest-Rate Smoothing," *Review of Economic Studies* 70, 861–886.

Woodford, M. (2003b): "Interest and Prices," Princeton University Press, Princeton, NJ.

Wu, J. C. and Xia, F. D. (2014): "Measuring the Macroeconomic Impact of Monetary Policy at the Zero Lower Bound," *NBER Working Paper Series* 20117, 1–55.

Yun, T. (1996): "Nominal Price Rigidity, Money Supply Endogeneity, and Business Cycles," *Journal of Monetary Economics* 37, 345–370.

Zietz, J. (2008): "A Clarifying Note on Converting to Log-Deviations from the Steady State," *Economics Bulletin* 3(50), 1–15.

Appendix

Contents

A.1 Generalized Mean

The original formula used in mathematics,

$$\bar{x} = \left(\frac{1}{n} \sum_{j=1}^{n} x_j^q \right)^{1/q}, \tag{A1}$$

can, for example, become the arithmetic mean for $q = 1$. Using $(\varepsilon - 1)/\varepsilon$ for q and writing it in integral form (with $n \to \infty$) gives

$$\bar{x} = \left(\int_0^1 x_j^{\frac{\varepsilon-1}{\varepsilon}} \, dj \right)^{\frac{\varepsilon}{\varepsilon-1}}, \tag{A2}$$

which can be utilized, as in Eq.(1), with consumption and ξ instead of j (due to the fact that $\xi \in \mathbb{R}$, an uncountable infinite set). The easiest way to examine the type of mean Eq.(1) can express is to use (A1) with limits 0 and 1 for q (one and infinity for ε respectively). It is much simpler for perfect substitutes ($\varepsilon \to \infty$) which become

$$\lim_{q \to 1} \left(\frac{1}{n} \sum_{j=1}^{n} x_j^q \right)^{1/q} = \frac{1}{n} \sum_{j=1}^{n} x_j, \tag{A3}$$

the arithmatic mean, as mentioned before. The case of perfect complements ($\varepsilon \to 1$) is a bit more complicated, since l'Hôpital's rule has to be used:

$$\begin{aligned} \lim_{q \to 0} \left(\frac{1}{n} \sum_{j=1}^{n} x_j^q \right)^{1/q} &= \lim_{q \to 0} \exp \left(\frac{\ln \left(\frac{1}{n} \sum x_j^q \right)}{q} \right) \overset{\text{"}\frac{0}{0}\text{"}}{=} \exp \left(\lim_{q \to 0} \frac{\frac{\frac{1}{n} \sum \ln(x_j) \cdot x_j^q}{\frac{1}{n} \sum x_j^q}}{1} \right) \\ &= \exp \left(\frac{\sum \ln(x_j) x_j^q}{\sum x_j^q} \right) = \exp \left(\frac{\sum \ln x_j}{n} \right) \\ &= \exp \left(\ln \left(\prod_{j=1}^{n} x_j^{1/n} \right) \right) = \left(\prod_{j=1}^{n} x_j \right)^{1/n}. \end{aligned} \tag{A4}$$

The aggregated consumption level can therefore vary between geometric (complements) and arithmetic mean (substitutes).

A.2 First-Order Condition of the Lagrangian Function (2)

Using the chain rule to obtain $\frac{\partial \mathscr{L}}{\partial C_\tau}$:

$$P_\tau - \lambda \frac{\varepsilon}{\varepsilon-1}\left(\int_0^1 C_\xi^{\frac{\varepsilon-1}{\varepsilon}}\, d\xi\right)^{\frac{\varepsilon}{\varepsilon-1}-1} \cdot \underbrace{\frac{\varepsilon-1}{\varepsilon} C_\tau^{\frac{\varepsilon-1}{\varepsilon}-1}}_{\text{derivative of sub-function}} = 0 \qquad \text{(A5.1)}$$

$$\Leftrightarrow \qquad P_\tau - \lambda\left(\int_0^1 C_\xi^{\frac{\varepsilon-1}{\varepsilon}}\, d\xi\right)^{\frac{1}{\varepsilon-1}} \cdot C_\tau^{-\frac{1}{\varepsilon}} = 0. \qquad \text{(A5.2)}$$

A.3 Rearranging the First-Order Condition (3.1)

First, exponentiate the integral with ε and $1/\varepsilon$. Then insert C from the constraint. It follows that

$$P_\tau = \lambda C_\tau^{-\frac{1}{\varepsilon}} C^{\frac{1}{\varepsilon}} \quad \Leftrightarrow \quad P_\tau = \lambda\left(\frac{C}{C_\tau}\right)^{\frac{1}{\varepsilon}} \qquad \text{(A6.1)}$$

$$\Leftrightarrow \quad \frac{P_\tau}{\lambda} = \left(\frac{C_\tau}{C}\right)^{-\frac{1}{\varepsilon}} \quad \Leftrightarrow \quad \left(\frac{P_\tau}{\lambda}\right)^{-\varepsilon} = \frac{C_\tau}{C}. \qquad \text{(A6.2)}$$

A.4 Rearranging to obtain Eq.(5)

Solve (4) for C_τ and insert the result for all firms in the constraint, Eq.(1):

$$C = \left(\int_0^1 \left(\left(\frac{P_\xi}{P}\right)^{-\varepsilon} C\right)^{\frac{\varepsilon-1}{\varepsilon}} d\xi\right)^{\frac{\varepsilon}{\varepsilon-1}} \Leftrightarrow C = \left(\frac{1}{P}\right)^{-\varepsilon} C \cdot \left(\int_0^1 P_\xi^{1-\varepsilon}\, d\xi\right)^{\frac{\varepsilon}{\varepsilon-1}} \qquad \text{(A7.1)}$$

$$\Leftrightarrow \quad P^{-\varepsilon} = \left(\int_0^1 P_\xi^{1-\varepsilon}\, d\xi\right)^{\frac{\varepsilon}{\varepsilon-1}} \quad \Leftrightarrow \quad P = \left(\int_0^1 P_\xi^{1-\varepsilon}\, d\xi\right)^{\frac{1}{1-\varepsilon}}. \qquad \text{(A7.2)}$$

A.5 Examining Eq.(5) with the Generalized Mean

The approach is the same as for the aggregated consumption level. Now, limits zero and negative infinity for q are used (for perfect complements and perfect substitutes respectively). As $q \to 0$ leads to the geometric mean, aggregated price and consumption levels behave indentically for perfect complements. Having $\varepsilon \to \infty$ leads to $P = \min\{P_\xi\}$, but since all prices have to be the same in this state, the arithmetic mean equals the minimum.

A.6 Growth Rates in Period t

$$z_t = \ln Z_t - \ln Z_{ss} = \ln Z_t - \ln Z_{t-1} + \ln Z_{t-1} - \ln Z_{ss}$$
$$= \ln(1 + \widetilde{z_t}) + \ln(1 + \widehat{z_{t-1}}) = \sum_{s=0}^{\infty} \ln(1 + \widetilde{z_{t-s}}) = \ln\left(\prod_{s=0}^{\infty}(1 + \widetilde{z_{t-s}})\right).$$

$$\Rightarrow \quad \widehat{z_t} = \prod_{s=0}^{\infty}(1 + \widetilde{z_{t-s}}) - 1, \tag{A8}$$

that is, with regard to GDP, the current output gap is the product of all GDP growth rates to date. The result shows that the iterated version of the output gap accounts for a cumulative growth. Thus

$$\ln(1 + \widehat{y_t}) = \ln(1 + \widetilde{y_t}) + \ln(1 + \widehat{y_{t-1}}) \tag{A9.1}$$
$$\Leftrightarrow \quad 1 + \widehat{y_t} = (1 + \widetilde{y_t})(1 + \widehat{y_{t-1}}) \tag{A9.2}$$
$$\Rightarrow \quad \widehat{y_t} \approx \widetilde{y_t} + \widehat{y_{t-1}} \tag{A9.3}$$

and

$$\ln(1 + \widehat{y_{t+1}}) = \ln(1 + \widetilde{y_{t+1}}) + \ln(1 + \widehat{y_t}) \tag{A10.1}$$
$$\Leftrightarrow \quad 1 + \widehat{y_{t+1}} = (1 + \widetilde{y_{t+1}})(1 + \widehat{y_t}) \tag{A10.2}$$
$$\Rightarrow \quad \widehat{y_{t+1}} \approx \widetilde{y_{t+1}} + \widehat{y_t}, \tag{A10.3}$$

so the current GDP growth rate can be approximated through the "gap" between the output gaps of current and previous periods.

A.7 Expected Duration of Resetting the Price in Calvo Pricing

$$1 \cdot (1 - \phi) + 2 \cdot \phi(1 - \phi) + 3 \cdot \phi^2(1 - \phi) + \ldots = \sum_{j=0}^{\infty}(j + 1) \cdot \phi^j(1 - \phi)$$
$$= (1 - \phi)\sum_{j=0}^{\infty}\left(\phi^{j+1}\right)'_{\phi} = (1 - \phi)\left(\sum_{j=0}^{\infty}\phi^{j+1}\right)'_{\phi} = (1 - \phi)\left(\phi\sum_{j=0}^{\infty}\phi^j\right)'_{\phi}$$
$$= (1 - \phi)\left(\frac{\phi}{1 - \phi}\right)'_{\phi} = (1 - \phi) \cdot \frac{(1 - \phi) + \phi}{(1 - \phi)^2} = \frac{1}{1 - \phi}. \tag{A11}$$

A higher share of firms unable to reset their price (in a certain period) increases the expected duration. In a Poisson process, the duration is exponentially distributed and thus $(E[X])^2 = Var[X]$ with the random variable X, the number of periods.

A.8 Examining the NKPC's Slope

The parameters defining κ determine the influence of $\widehat{y}_t$ on π_t in the NKPC, where the term *influence* accounts for both scenarios, an inflationary and a recessionary gap. The following applies: $\varepsilon > 1$ (elasticity of substitution), $\gamma > 0$ (cost parameter, i.e. the slope of marginal costs' log deviations from their long-run trend values), $0 < \beta < 1$ (discount parameter, i.e. time preference), and $0 < \phi < 1$ (share of *sticky prices*). Recalling $\kappa = \gamma(1-\phi)(1-\beta\phi)/((1+\varepsilon\gamma)\phi) > 0$, the partial derivatives are

$$\frac{\partial\kappa}{\partial\varepsilon} = \frac{\gamma(1-\phi)(1-\beta\phi)}{\phi}\cdot\frac{-\gamma}{(1+\varepsilon\gamma)^2} = \frac{-\gamma^2(1-\phi)(1-\beta\phi)}{(1+\varepsilon\gamma)^2\phi} = -\frac{\gamma}{1+\varepsilon\gamma}\kappa \quad < 0 \qquad \text{(A12.1)}$$

$$\frac{\partial\kappa}{\partial\gamma} = \frac{(1-\phi)(1-\beta\phi)}{\phi}\cdot\frac{(1+\varepsilon\gamma)-\gamma\varepsilon}{(1+\varepsilon\gamma)^2} = \frac{\gamma(1-\phi)(1-\beta\phi)}{(1+\varepsilon\gamma)^2\phi} = \frac{1}{1+\varepsilon\gamma}\kappa \quad > 0 \qquad \text{(A12.2)}$$

$$\frac{\partial\kappa}{\partial\beta} = \frac{\gamma(1-\phi)}{(1+\varepsilon\gamma)\phi}\cdot(-\phi) = \frac{-\gamma(1-\phi)}{1+\varepsilon\gamma} = -\frac{\phi}{1-\beta\phi}\kappa \quad < 0 \qquad \text{(A12.3)}$$

$$\begin{aligned}\frac{\partial\kappa}{\partial\phi} &= \frac{\gamma}{1+\varepsilon\gamma}\cdot\frac{(-(1-\beta\phi)+(1-\phi)(-\beta))\phi-(1-\phi)(1-\beta\phi)}{\phi^2}\\ &= \frac{\gamma}{1+\varepsilon\gamma}\cdot\frac{-(1-\beta\phi)-\beta\phi(1-\phi)}{\phi} = \frac{\gamma}{1+\varepsilon\gamma}\cdot\frac{\beta\phi^2-1}{\phi} = -\frac{1-\beta\phi^2}{1-\beta\phi}\kappa < 0. \qquad \text{(A12.4)}\end{aligned}$$

Higher values for ε, β, and ϕ have a negative impact on the NKPC's slope, whereas higher values for γ have a positive impact.

Competitive markets, product variety, and substitutes (large ε) slow down the inflation but monopolies (small ε) favor price increases. High production costs (large γ) will be passed on through price increases by the firms. Due to the importance of future losses (large β), firms choose a price path (x_t) with higher deviations from the optimal price path (p_t^*). β also has an effect through the expected inflation term ($E_t\pi_{t+1}$). A high importance attached to the future (large β) results in a higher impact of $E_t\pi_{t+1}$ on today's inflation. In addition, the influence of changes in β through expectations is larger than through the output gap since $\frac{\partial\kappa}{\partial\beta} \in]-1,0[$ (with (A12.3)):

$$0 > \frac{\gamma(\phi-1)}{1+\varepsilon\gamma} > \lim_{\varepsilon\to1}\lim_{\phi\to0}\frac{\gamma(\phi-1)}{1+\varepsilon\gamma} = \frac{-\gamma}{1+\gamma} > \lim_{\gamma\to\infty}\frac{-\gamma}{1+\gamma} = -1. \qquad \text{(A13)}$$

When a small number of firms have the possibility to adjust the price in period t (large ϕ), there is only a small chance to belong to this share. For this reason, firms choose a price path (x_t) with higher deviations from the optimal price path (p_t^*).

A.9 Reduced-Form NKPC without Log-Linearization

$$\pi_t = \beta E_t \pi_{t+1} + \kappa \widehat{y_t} \tag{A14.1}$$

$$\Rightarrow \quad \ln(1+\pi_t) = \beta \ln(1 + E_t\pi_{t+1}) + \kappa \ln(1+\widehat{y_t}) \tag{A14.2}$$

$$\Leftrightarrow \quad \ln(1+\pi_t) = \ln\left((1+E_t\pi_{t+1})^{\beta} \cdot (1+\widehat{y_t})^{\kappa}\right) \tag{A14.3}$$

$$\Leftrightarrow \quad \pi_t = (1+E_t\pi_{t+1})^{\beta} \cdot (1+\widehat{y_t})^{\kappa} - 1 \tag{A14.4}$$

Optionally with GDP growth rates:

$$\Leftrightarrow \quad \pi_t = (1+E_t\pi_{t+1})^{\beta} \cdot \left(\prod_{s=0}^{\infty}(1+\widetilde{y_{t-s}})\right)^{\kappa} - 1 \tag{A15.1}$$

$$\Leftrightarrow \quad \pi_t = (1+E_t\pi_{t+1})^{\beta} \cdot \prod_{s=0}^{\infty}(1+\widetilde{y_{t-s}})^{\kappa} - 1. \tag{A15.2}$$

In a MATLAB simulation (with $\beta = 0.99$, $\kappa = 0.04$, and $E_t\pi_{t+1} = 0.02$) the inflation rate can be both under- and overestimated depending on $\widehat{y_t}$. Figures A1 and A2 show this.

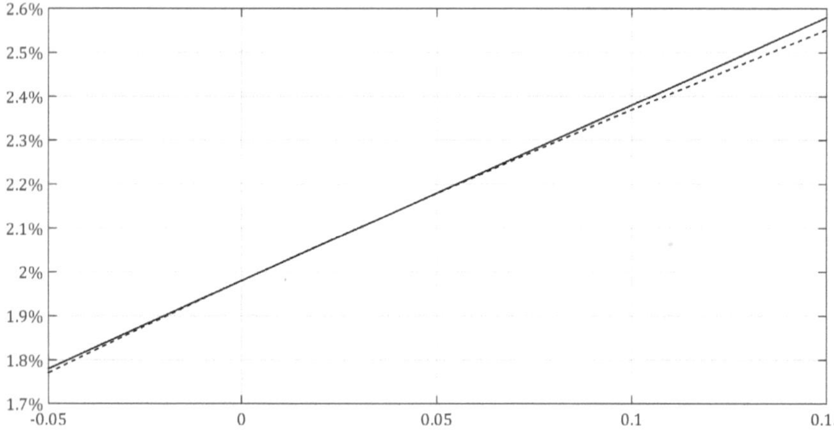

Figure A1: Linear NKPC (black) and NKPC without log-linearization (dashed). Horizontal axis: output gap growth rate $\widehat{y_t}$. Vertical axis: inflation rate π_t.

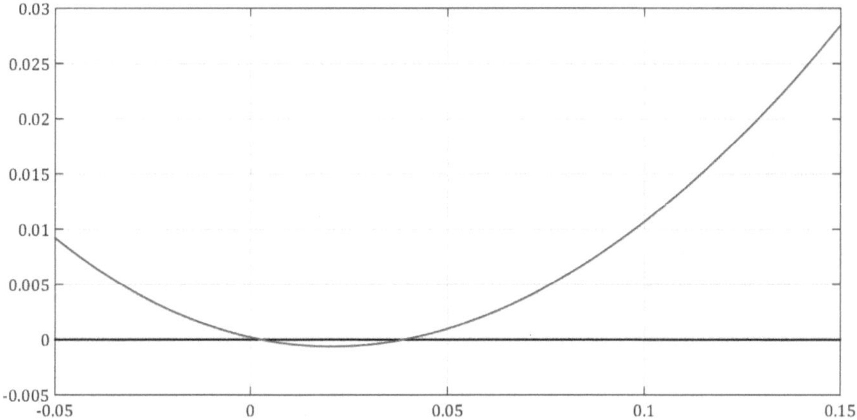

Figure A2: Differences of both curves in Figure A1. The growth rate is underestimated between slightly over 0% and 4% and therefore, in most cases, since growth rates in developed countries are usually in this range. Horizontal axis: output gap growth rate $\widehat{y}_t$. Vertical axis: inflation rate π_t in basis points. Note that on the vertical axis, an interval of 0.01 corresponds to a hundredth of one percentage of inflation.

A.10 Intertemporal Optimization via Dynamic Programming

Dynamic Programming uses the additively separable utility function and the envelope theorem to set up optimality conditions for two consecutive periods. The procedure can be divided into three parts. The first part is to write a value function named after Bellman (1957). Under the assumption that the second term of the expanded utility

$$U(C_t) + E_t\left[\sum_{s=t+1}^{\infty} \beta^{s-t-1} U(C_s)\right] \tag{A16}$$

is maximized in period t, the Bellman equation is

$$V(B_t) \equiv \max_{C_t} \{U(C_t) + \beta V(B_{t+1})\}\,. \tag{A17}$$

The expected value vanishes since B_{t+1} is determined by variables in period t in the constraint. Differentiating with respect to C_t gives the first-order condition

$$\frac{d}{dC_t}U(C_t) + \beta\frac{d}{dC_t}V(B_{t+1}) = U'(C_t) + \beta V'(B_{t+1}) \cdot \frac{dB_{t+1}}{dC_t} = 0, \tag{A18}$$

which results in

$$U'(C_t) = P_t \beta V'(B_{t+1}). \tag{A19}$$

Eq.(A19) relates the marginal utility to the marginal value in the following period, the time preference, and prices in the same period. Therefore, a higher β and P_t results in a lower C_t.

In the next part, the envelope theorem is used to differentiate the value function (by inserting the optimized C_t^*) with respect to the costate variable B_t:

$$V(B_t) = U(C_t^*) + \beta V(B_{t+1}) \tag{A20.1}$$

$$\Rightarrow \quad \frac{dV}{dB_t} = \beta V'(B_{t+1}) \cdot \frac{dB_{t+1}}{dB_t} \tag{A20.2}$$

$$\Leftrightarrow \quad V'(B_t) = \beta V'(B_{t+1}) \cdot (1 + i_{t-1}). \tag{A20.3}$$

Eq.(A20.3) reveals the relationship of the marginal value functions.

In a third and last step, the first-order condition (A19) can be used to replace the value functions in Eq.(A20.3) with the marginal utility in both periods t and $t-1$:

$$\frac{U'(C_{t-1})}{P_{t-1}\beta} = \beta \cdot \frac{U'(C_t)}{P_t \beta} \cdot (1 + i_{t-1}) \tag{A21.1}$$

$$\Rightarrow \quad \frac{U'(C_t)}{P_t} = \beta(1 + i_t)\frac{E_t[U'(C_{t+1})]}{E_t[P_{t+1}]}. \tag{A21.2}$$

The time shift yields the Euler condition. Thus, the relationships apply for all periods when solving forward:

$$U'(C_t) = \beta(1+i_t)\frac{P_t}{E_t[P_{t+1}]} \cdot E_t\left[\beta(1+i_{t+1})\frac{P_{t+1}}{E_t[P_{t+2}]} \cdot E_{t+1}[U'(C_{t+2})]\right] \tag{A22.1}$$

$$= E_t\left[(1+i_t)(1+i_{t+1})\beta^2 \frac{P_t P_{t+1}}{P_{t+1}P_{t+2}} U'(C_{t+2})\right] \tag{A22.2}$$

$$= E_t\left[\prod_{j=0}^{n-1}(1+i_{t+j})\beta^n \frac{P_t}{P_{t+n}} U'(C_{t+n})\right] \tag{A22.3}$$

$$= \beta^n P_t E_t\left[\prod_{j=0}^{n-1}(1+i_{t+j}) P_{t+n}^{-1} U'(C_{t+n})\right]. \tag{A22.4}$$

A.11 Intertemporal Elasticity of Substitution in (39)

The IES is defined as the percentage change of the intertemporal consumption ratio (C_{t+1}/C_t) to a one percentage increase of the accumulation factor $(1+i_t)$. The latter corresponds to the interest rate's increase of one percentage point for small values of i_t. Plugging the marignal utility in the Euler equation and solving for the consumption ratio gives

$$\frac{C_{t+1}}{C_t} = (1+i_t)^{-\sigma}\left(\beta\frac{P_t}{E[P_{t+1}]}\right)^{-\sigma}, \tag{A23}$$

with $1/\sigma$ as the elasticity.

A.12 Reduced-Form IS Curve without Log-Linearization

Point of entry is (40), then taking logs, and expressing in growth rates:

$$\beta(1+i_t) = E_t\left[\frac{P_{t+1}}{P_t}\cdot\frac{Y_{t+1}^{\sigma}}{Y_t^{\sigma}}\right] \tag{A24.1}$$

$$= E_t\left[\exp(\ln(1+\pi_{t+1}) + \sigma\ln(1+\widetilde{y_{t+1}})\right] \tag{A24.2}$$

$$= E_t[(1+\pi_{t+1})(1+\widetilde{y_{t+1}})^{\sigma}]. \tag{A24.3}$$

There is no connection between i_t and $\widehat{y_t}$, but GDP growth rates from t to $t+1$ are necessary when working with data. Again, this time with output gaps:

$$\beta(1+i_t) = E_t\left[\exp(\ln(1+\pi_{t+1}) + \sigma\ln(1+\widehat{y_{t+1}}) - \sigma\ln(1+\widehat{y_t}))\right] \tag{A25.1}$$

$$= (1+\widehat{y_t})^{-\sigma}E_t\left[(1+\pi_{t+1})(1+\widehat{y_{t+1}})^{\sigma}\right] \tag{A25.2}$$

$$\Leftrightarrow \quad (1+\widehat{y_t})^{\sigma} = \frac{E_t\left[(1+\pi_{t+1})(1+\widehat{y_{t+1}})^{\sigma}\right]}{\beta(1+i_t)} \tag{A25.3}$$

With β:

$$\widehat{y_t} = \left(\frac{E_t\left[(1+\pi_{t+1})(1+\widehat{y_{t+1}})^{\sigma}\right]}{\beta(1+i_t)}\right)^{1/\sigma} - 1. \tag{A26}$$

With r:

$$\widehat{y_t} = \left(\frac{E_t\left[(1+\pi_{t+1})(1+\widehat{y_{t+1}})^{\sigma}\right](1+r)}{1+i_t}\right)^{1/\sigma} - 1. \tag{A27}$$

$\widehat{y_t}(i_t)$ as a function is convex and takes the shape of a hyperbola. A vertical IS curve arises for $1/\sigma \rightarrow 0$. The dynamic IS curve, Eq.(45), noticably shows that the current output now depends solely on the expected output. Figure A3 illustrates both shapes.

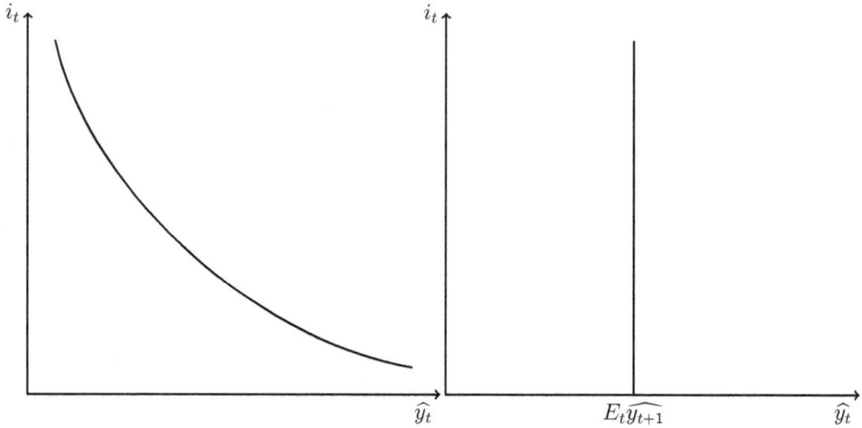

Figure A3: IS curve (i) without log-linearization and (ii) an investment trap type case.

The second derivative can be examined to determine the quality of approximation:

$$\frac{\partial \widehat{y_t}}{\partial i_t} = -\frac{1}{\sigma} \cdot \frac{\widehat{y_t} + 1}{1 + i_t} \tag{A28.1}$$

$$\frac{\partial^2 \widehat{y_t}}{\partial i_t^2} = \frac{1 + \sigma}{\sigma^2} \cdot \frac{\widehat{y_t} + 1}{(1 + i_t)^2} \tag{A28.2}$$

With $1 + i_t = (1 + r)(1 + E_t \pi_{t+1})$, the Fisher equation, yields

$$\widehat{y_t} = \left(\frac{E_t\left[(1 + \pi_{t+1})(1 + \widehat{y_{t+1}})^{\sigma}\right]}{1 + E_t \pi_{t+1}} \right)^{-\sigma} - 1. \tag{A29}$$

If everyone expects $\widehat{y_{t+1}} = 0$, then $\widehat{y_t} = 0$ holds true.

A.13 Proof of the Conditions for a Unique Equilibrium

To find both necessary and sufficient conditions, the eigenvalues of the 2×2 matrix M have to be inside the unit circle. Since the matrix only has two columns and rows, the p/q-formula can be used and the characteristic polynom includes the trace and the determinant of M. The following equation has to be solved for complex numbers:

$$\lambda^2 - Tr(M)\lambda + Det(M) = 0, \tag{A30}$$

where $Tr(M)$ is the trace, the sum of elements on the main diagonal, and $Det(M)$ the determinant of M. To solve for λ, the following applies:

$$\lambda_{1/2} = \frac{Tr(M)}{2} \pm \sqrt{\left(\frac{Tr(M)}{2}\right)^2 - Det(M)}. \tag{A31}$$

Case 1: $\lambda_{1/2}$ are real $\Leftrightarrow$ $Tr^2(M) > 4 \cdot Det(M)$.
Case 1.1 is

$$\frac{Tr(M)}{2} + \sqrt{\left(\frac{Tr(M)}{2}\right)^2 - Det(M)} < 1 \tag{A32.1}$$

$$\Leftrightarrow \quad \left(\frac{Tr(M)}{2}\right)^2 - Det(M) < \left(1 - \frac{Tr(M)}{2}\right)^2 \tag{A32.2}$$

$$\Leftrightarrow \quad -Det(M) < 1 - Tr(M) \tag{A32.3}$$

$$\Leftrightarrow \quad Tr(M) < 1 + Det(M). \tag{A32.4}$$

Case 1.2 is analog

$$\frac{Tr(M)}{2} - \sqrt{\left(\frac{Tr(M)}{2}\right)^2 - Det(M)} > -1 \tag{A33.1}$$

$$\Leftrightarrow \quad -Tr(M) < 1 + Det(M). \tag{A33.2}$$

Both subcases lead to condition (59.2).
Case 2: $\lambda_1 = \lambda_2$ $\Leftrightarrow$ $Tr^2(M) = 4 \cdot Det(M)$.

Only the first term is to be taken into account. The condition is

$$\left|\frac{Tr(M)}{2}\right| < 1. \tag{A34}$$

Case 3: $\lambda_{1/2}$ are imaginary $\Leftrightarrow$ $Tr^2(M) < 4 \cdot Det(M)$.
Written as complex number, the formula is

$$\lambda_{1/2} = \frac{Tr(M)}{2} \pm \sqrt{Det(M) - \left(\frac{Tr(M)}{2}\right)^2} \cdot i, \tag{A35}$$

with $i = \sqrt{-1}$.
Case 3.1 is

$$\frac{Tr(M)}{2} + \sqrt{Det(M) - \left(\frac{Tr(M)}{2}\right)^2} \cdot i \tag{A36.1}$$

$$\Rightarrow \quad \left|\frac{Tr(M)}{2}\right| < 1 \wedge \sqrt{Det(M) - \left(\frac{Tr(M)}{2}\right)^2} < 1 \tag{A36.2}$$

$$\Leftrightarrow \quad \left|\frac{Tr(M)}{2}\right| < 1 \wedge Det(M) - \left(\frac{Tr(M)}{2}\right)^2 < 1. \tag{A36.3}$$

Case 3.2 (analog to 1.2) will have the same result as 3.1.

Case 3 implies case 2. Both conditions in case 3.1 lead to condition (59.1).

A.14 System of Equations in Matrix Form

Inserting the general forward-looking Taylor rule, Eq.(60), into the IS curve gives

$$\widehat{y_t} = E_t\widehat{y_{t+1}} - \frac{1}{\sigma}(\alpha_y E_t\widehat{y_{t+1}} + \alpha_\pi E_t\pi_{t+1} - E_t\pi_{t+1}) + u_t. \tag{A37}$$

Using $\alpha_y = \sigma$ and replacing $\widehat{y_t}$ in the NKPC yields

$$\pi_t = \beta E_t\pi_{t+1} + \kappa\left((1-\alpha_\pi)\sigma^{-1}E_t\pi_{t+1} + u_t\right) + e_t \tag{A38}$$

and rearranging with the first equation:

$$\widehat{y_t} = 0 \cdot E_t\widehat{y_{t+1}} \qquad (1-\alpha_\pi)\sigma^{-1}E_t\pi_{t+1} + u_t \tag{A39.1}$$

$$\pi_t = 0 \cdot E_t\widehat{y_{t+1}} + \left(\beta + \kappa(1-\alpha_\pi)\sigma^{-1}\right)E_t\pi_{t+1} + \kappa u_t + e_t. \tag{A39.2}$$

Bringing both in matrix form:

$$\begin{bmatrix}\widehat{y_t}\\ \pi_t\end{bmatrix} = \begin{bmatrix}0 & (1-\alpha_\pi)\sigma^{-1}\\ 0 & \beta + \kappa(1-\alpha_\pi)\sigma^{-1}\end{bmatrix} \cdot \begin{bmatrix}E_t\widehat{y_{t+1}}\\ E_t\pi_{t+1}\end{bmatrix} + \begin{bmatrix}u_t\\ \kappa u_t + e_t\end{bmatrix}. \tag{A40}$$

A.15 Second-Order Taylor Approximation

The Taylor series (in $\mathbb{R}$) helps in finding a polynomial to substitute a certain function $f(x)$ (i.e. exponential, logarithm, etc.) around a point x_0. The generalized formula of the degree n in the compact sigma notation is

$$Taylor(n) = \sum_{j=0}^{n} \frac{f^{(j)}(x_0)}{j!}(x - x_0)^j, \tag{A41}$$

where $f^{(j)}$ denotes the jth derivative with $f^{(0)} = f$ as a special case. Thereby, larger values for n give better approximations of the original function $f(x)$. In (84.1), $f(x) = \ln(1 + x)$ and $n = 2$. Formula (A41) simplifies to

$$Taylor(2) = \ln(1 + x_0) + \frac{1}{1 + x_0}(x - x_0) - \frac{1}{2(1 + x_0)^2}(x - x_0)^2. \tag{A42}$$

The result in (84.1) appears with $x_0 = 0$ and $\widetilde{y_{t+1}}$ (π_{t+1} respectively) as the argument of the function:

$$\ln(1 + \widetilde{y_{t+1}}) \approx \widetilde{y_{t+1}} - \frac{1}{2}\widetilde{y_{t+1}}^2. \tag{A43}$$

A.16 Quadratic Approximation in Bauer and Neuenkirch (2015)

Log-linearizing Eq.(40) gives:

$$\frac{1 + r}{1 + i_t} = E_t(\exp(-\pi_{t+1} - \sigma\widetilde{y_{t+1}})) \tag{A44.1}$$

$$\Leftrightarrow \quad 1 + r - i \approx E_t\left[1 - \pi_{t+1} - \sigma\widetilde{y_{t+1}} + \frac{1}{2}\left(\pi_{t+1} + \sigma\widetilde{y_{t+1}}\right)^2\right] \tag{A44.2}$$

$$\Leftrightarrow \quad r - i \approx -E_t\pi_{t+1} - \sigma E_t\widehat{y_{t+1}} + \sigma\widehat{y_t} + \frac{1}{2}E_t(\ldots)^2 \tag{A44.3}$$

$$\Leftrightarrow \quad -\sigma\widehat{y_t} = -\sigma E_t\widehat{y_{t+1}} + i_t - r - E_t\pi_{t+1} + \frac{1}{2}E_t(\ldots)^2 \tag{A44.4}$$

$$\Leftrightarrow \quad \widehat{y_t} = E_t\widehat{y_{t+1}} - \frac{1}{\sigma}(i_t - r - E_t\pi_{t+1}) - \frac{1}{2\sigma}E_t(\ldots)^2. \tag{A44.5}$$

After multiplying, the quadratic IS curve takes the form of

$$\widehat{y_t} = E_t\widehat{y_{t+1}} - \frac{1}{\sigma}(i_t - r - E_t\pi_{t+1}) - \frac{1}{2\sigma}E_t\pi_{t+1}^2 - \frac{\sigma}{2}E_t\widetilde{y_{t+1}}^2 - \sigma E_t[\pi_{t+1}\widetilde{y_{t+1}}]. \tag{A45}$$

A.17 Basis Point Difference in Special Cases

Depicted are the cases of strict inflation targeting and without persistence.

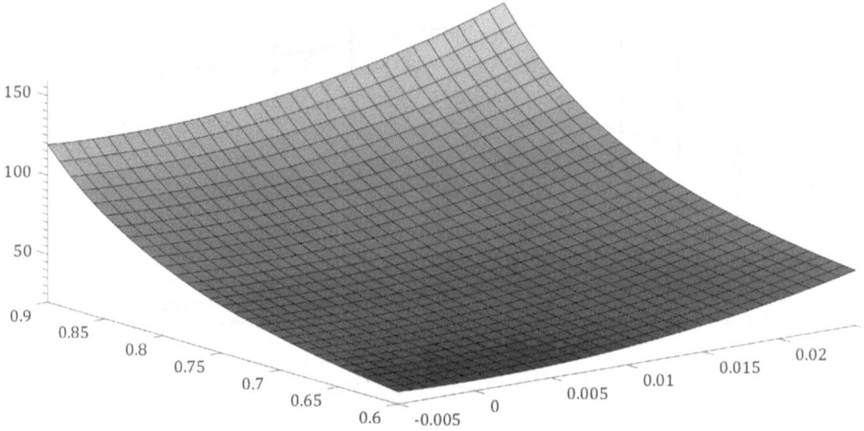

Figure A4: Differences between both cases (with and without uncertainty) in the equilibrium condition with strict inflation targeting. Horizontal axes: Persistence μ and cost shock e_t. Vertical axis: Difference of interest rate i_t.

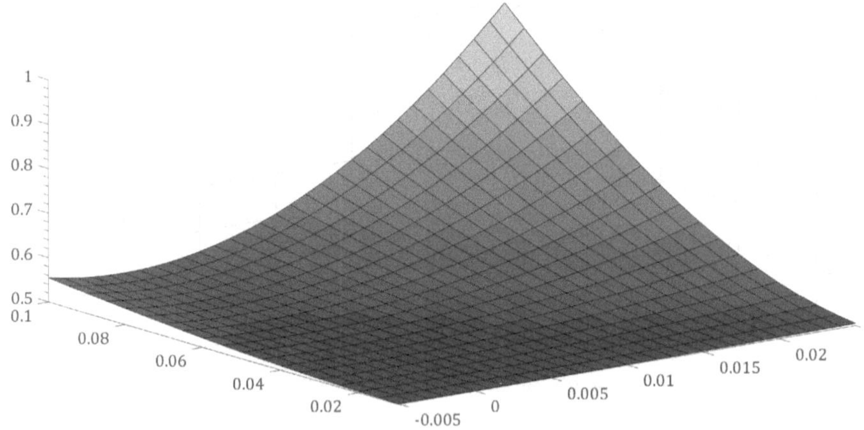

Figure A5: Differences between both cases (with and without uncertainty) in the equilibrium condition without persistence. Horizontal axes: NKPC's slope κ and cost shock e_t. Vertical axis: Difference of interest rate i_t in basis points.

Figure A4 shows similar differences as the main result in Section 4.5, whereas Figure A5 shows that without persistence uncertainty plays practically no role.

A.18 Additional Scenarios

Depicted are scenarios, similar to Subsection 4.6, with a σ, δ, and σ_e^2 variable.

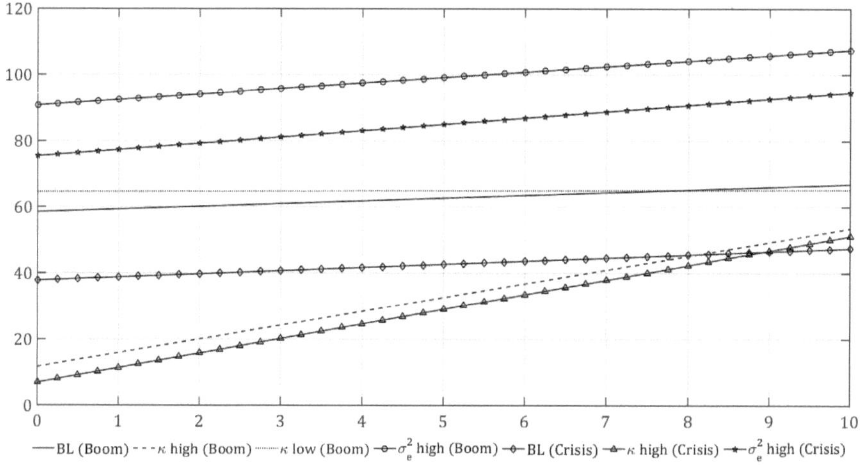

Figure A6: Difference of i_t in several scenarios when σ is variable. Horizontal axis: Reciprocal value of the IES σ. Vertical axis: Difference of interest rate i_t in basis points.

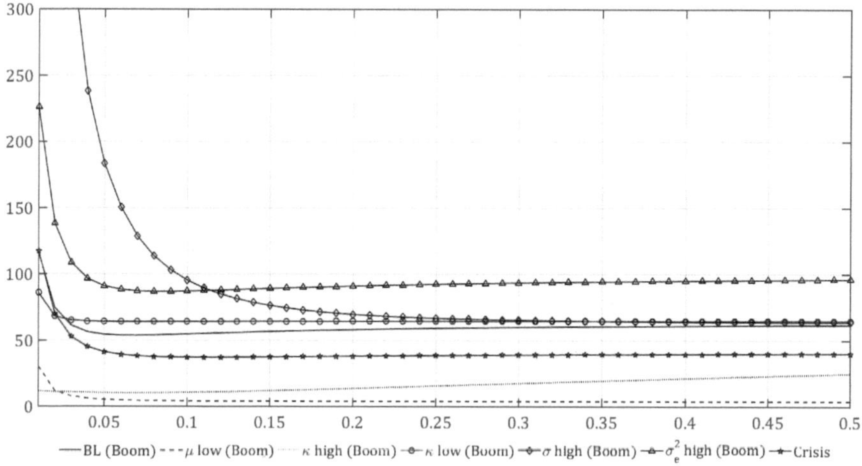

Figure A7: Difference of i_t in several scenarios when δ is variable. Horizontal axis: Weight on output fluctuations δ. Vertical axis: Difference of interest rate i_t in basis points.

The interest rate difference decreases with higher IES in Figure A6. The same holds true for the weight on output fluctuations in Figure A7, only that the basis point level is more or less constant at a certain point. In Figure A8, the impact of uncertainty constantly increases for a larger cost shock variance.

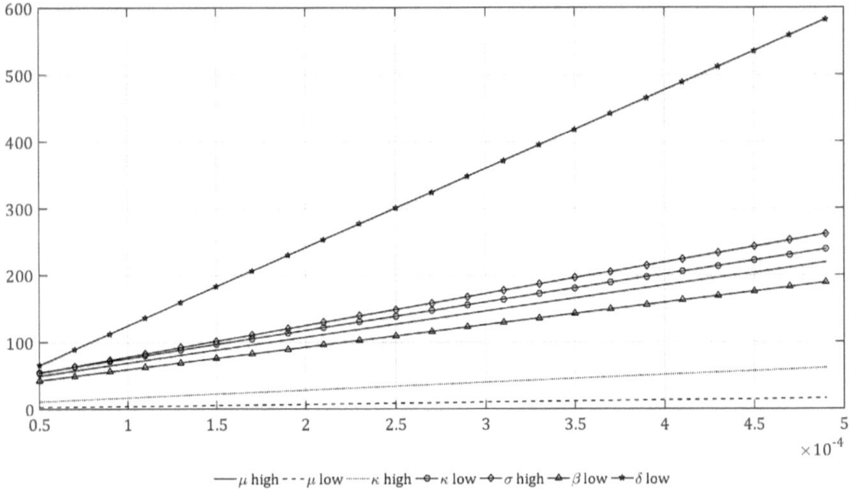

Figure A8: Difference of i_t in several scenarios when σ_e^2 is variable. Horizontal axis: Cost shock variance σ_e^2. Vertical axis: Difference of interest rate i_t in basis points.